Child Support in the UK

Reassessing the issues

Edited by Bridget Pettitt

CPAG, 1-5 Bath Street, London EC1V 9PY

CPAG promotes action for the relief, directly or indirectly, of poverty among children and families with children. We work to ensure that those on low incomes get their full entitlements to welfare benefits. In our campaigning and information work we seek to improve benefits and policies for low-income families, in order to eradicate the injustice of poverty. If you are not already supporting us, please consider making a donation or ask for details of our membership schemes and publications.

This book is published in association with Save the Children. Save the Children works in the UK and across the world. Emergency relief runs alongside long-term development and prevention work to help children, their families and communities to be self-sufficient. We learn from the reality of children's lives and campaign for solutions to the problems they face. We gain experience through our projects around the world and use that knowledge to educate and advise others.

Poverty Publication 98

Published by Child Poverty Action Group
1–5 Bath Street, London EC1V 9PY

© Child Poverty Action Group 1998
Company No 1993854
Registered Charity No 294841

ISBN 1 901698 13 0

The views expressed in this book are the authors' and do not necessarily express those of CPAG.

A CIP record for this book is available from the British Library.

Cover and design by Devious Designs 0114 275 5634
Cover photographs by Paula Solloway/Format (front) and Jenny Matthews/Format (back)
Typeset by Nancy White 0171 607 4510
Printed by Progressive Printing UK Ltd 01702 520050

CONTENTS

ACKNOWLEDGEMENTS

This publication arose from a seminar held by Save the Children and Child Poverty Action Group in December 1996. I would like to thank Lisa Harker, formerly of CPAG, for devising and running the seminar and for her early work on the book. I would also like to thank the participants of the seminar for their contributions and assistance: Bharti Patel, Low Pay Unit; Susan Brighouse, CPAG; Patti Hill, Child Employment Network; Ben Whitney; Ginny Morrow, London School of Economics; Madeleine Leonard, Queens University, Belfast; Sandy Hobbs, University of Paisley; Carol Nevison, Sophie Laws, and Rachel Marcus, all from Save the Children.

I am extremely grateful to the readers of the book – Paula Rodgers, Terri MacDermott, Gerison Landsdown and, particularly, Rachel Marcus and Chris Cuninghame for their very constructive comments and support. Thanks also to Frances Ellery for copy editing and co-ordinating production of the book, to Nancy White for typesetting it, to Paula McDiarmid for proofreading and to Save the Children colleagues including Bill Bell, Sheri Chamberlain, Caroline Harper, Sophie Laws, Madeleine Parkyn, Angela Penrose, Caroline Pook and Madeleine Tearse.

Bridget Pettitt
Save the Children
June 1998

BIOGRAPHIES

THE EDITOR

Bridget Pettitt is Regional Research Officer for UK and Europe, Save the Children. She participated in and co-ordinated the SCF research on children's perspective of work in the UK.

THE CONTRIBUTORS

Sandy Hobbs is Reader in Psychology at the University of Paisley. **Jim McKechnie** is Senior Lecturer in Psychology at the University of Paisley. They have been conducting research on child employment on behalf of local authorities and other bodies for several years. They are co-authors of *Child Employment in Britain: A Social and Psychological Analysis* (Stationery Office, 1997) and joint editors of *Working Children: Reconsidering the Debates* (1998), the final report of the International Working Group on Child Labour. **Sandra Lindsay** was formerly a Research Assistant in Child Labour at the University of Paisley.

Michael Lavalette is lecturer in Social Policy at the University of Liverpool.

Sue Middleton is Senior Research Fellow and Director of the Lifestyles and Living Standards Programme at the Centre for Research in Social Policy, Loughborough University. She has researched and written extensively on children's living standards. **Jules Shropshire** is currently a Research Associate at the Centre for Research in Social Policy, Loughborough University. **Nicola Croden** is currently an undergraduate student studying sociology at Surrey University. She joined the Centre for Research and Social Policy, Loughborough University in 1996 for one year, where she was involved in research examining children's lifestyles and living standards.

Ruth Campbell is a Research and Development Officer for Save the Children based in Edinburgh. **Chris Cuninghame** is a Research Officer for Save the Children in London. **Carol Nevison** is a Research and Development Officer for Save the Children based in Newcastle. **Paula Rodgers** is Research and Policy Manager for

Save the Children in Belfast, and **Suzanne Mooney** is a Development Officer for Save the Children in Belfast.

Madeleine Leonard is a lecturer in the Department of Sociology and Social Policy at Queen's University Belfast where she teaches Development Studies. She is currently engaged in research commissioned by Save the Children in Belfast into term time employment among fifteen-year-old school students in Belfast.

Ellen Heptinstall is a Research Associate at Thomas Coram Research Unit. Recently she wrote a report on young people and their accidents at work for the Child Accident Prevention Trust (CAPT).

Norman Barton is Headteacher, and **Shirley Horton** is the Careers Education Co-ordinator, at Peele School, Long Sutton.

Rachel Marcus is a Research Officer based in London for Save the Children. She has researched and written on child labour issues in the international context, and recently led a research project on child labour in the football industry in Pakistan.

Ben Whitney is Education Welfare Specialist Officer for Staffordshire LEA, Honorary Research Fellow at Staffordshire University and a writer/trainer on education social work issues. He is responsible for the county's child employment system and supports schools in their child protection responsibilities.

Introduction

Bridget Pettitt

The issue of children working is complex. It raises fundamental questions about our notions of childhood and children's role in society. Children's employment is affected by, and contributes to, the changing economic structure of the labour force. The fact that children work challenges also our concept of the role of education. This complexity is reflected in divergent attitudes towards children working in the UK. At one extreme it is seen as an example of the worst form of exploitation of the most vulnerable section of society. At the other extreme there is a widespread denial that children are working in any meaningful way, other than working for pocket money. This confusion has led, on the one hand, to a lack of interest in children's work until recently, and, on the other, to the creation of ambiguous and contradictory policies and legislation. More often than not, the children and young people themselves are left out of the debate entirely.

For several reasons the employment of children is now on the political agenda. Although many organisations have been long concerned with this issue,[1] recent interest has its roots in the increase in international attention to child labour, the children's rights movement and new thinking about the role of children in society.

There has been increased interest in the issues on a global scale. People in the 'developed' countries are becoming more aware of the exploitation of children in 'developing' countries and the part they themselves play as consumers.[2] This has led to an increased interest in the issue on their own doorstep. Recent policy initiatives and legislation have reflected this international concern – for example, the International Labour Organisation (ILO) is developing a new Convention which bans the most extreme and harmful work for children, and is campaigning actively for the ratification of ILO Convention 138 – The Minimum Age Convention. In 1994, the EU produced a Directive on the Employment of Children which aims to standardise the age at which children can work, the number of hours and the nature of their work. Most recently, a Private Members Bill on children's work was debated in the UK Parliament. The Government is currently conducting a governmental review of the regulation of child employment.

Much of this debate on children's employment comes from a concern about children's well being. However, the debate has also been driven by concerns about the effect of child employment on the labour market. The employment of children is clearly a children's rights issue. Article 32 of the United Nations Convention on the Rights of the Child (CRC) states that children have a right to protection from economic exploitation. In addition, the best interests of the child should be a paramount principle in all decisions taken about children's lives (Article 3) and children have a right to be consulted on issues affecting them (Article 12).

The CRC has developed in the context of new thinking around children and childhood and their role in society.[3] This has challenged the notion of children as dependent members of society. There has been a move to look at children as active social and economic participants – as workers rather than as passive consumers.

WHAT ARE THE MAIN ISSUES RELATED TO CHILDREN WORKING IN THE UK?

- **Nature and extent:** How extensive a phenomenon is it – how many children work, at what age? What kind of work are children doing? What information do we have about the nature of children's work in the UK?
- **Children's perspective:** What does the work that children do mean to them and how do they fit it into their lives? What do children think about the work they do? What motivates them to work and what do they do with their earnings? What is the reality for children who work in the 1990s?
- **Healthy or harmful?** Is the work that children are doing harmful or is it healthy? What is the relationship between education and

part-time work? What do we know about the more extreme forms of working – eg, prostitution or drug running. Should these indeed be considered as work?

- **Issues of difference:** What are the impacts of gender, disability and ethnicity on children's experience of work? What is the impact of social exclusion and living in areas of high unemployment on children's experience of work?
- **Poverty:** What is the relationship between poverty and children's work? Clearly the historical development of children's work has been closely related to the mode of production and to poverty. What is this relationship in the 1990s? Do more children from poorer families work than affluent children? Are their reasons and motivation for working different? Is the context of their work different – do they do different jobs? What is the economic impact of children's work more generally on the UK economy?
- **Domestic work:** What is the relationship between children's work, family economy and domestic work?
- **Action:** What action is required to ensure that children's rights are upheld to prevent their exploitation, danger to their health, education or development, while ensuring their participation in the debate? How can we ensure that children are protected from harmful and exploitative forms of work? What can be learnt from international experience of the child labour issue? How can we ensure that the work children do is beneficial to them?

The aim of this book is to answer some of these questions, and to provide pointers where more research and debate is needed. Save the Children (SCF) and Child Poverty Action Group (CPAG) are particularly concerned with the issues of poverty, marginalisation and exploitation. SCF has been campaigning and working on the issue of children who work in countries throughout the developing world and in the UK. This book takes a child focused approach to the issues, and brings children's own perspectives into the debate.

This volume, however, cannot hope to cover all the issues. Some key players in the debate are not represented here. The voices of employers themselves and parents of working children are missing, as are those trade unions which have been active campaigners on the issue. There has been little research on the specific issues facing children from minority ethnic groups who work and this gap is reflected here.[4] Where possible, conclusions about gender patterns have been drawn out, but again there is a lack of analysis of this in the available literature. Mention of disability issues is also scarce, both in terms of disabled children's experience of work and the impact which disability might have within the family.[5]

This book focuses on the more formal work that children are involved in, but there are other areas of children's work that remain invisible, such as work in the informal sector, and the work of very young children. These gaps notwithstanding, the information in this text will be of practical use to policy-makers in the UK who are seeking to improve the situation for working children in this country.

Various definitions of 'work' and of 'children' are used throughout the debate on children and work. Some define 'work' as paid work outside the family (which excludes paid work *within* the family, such as cleaning cars). It also excludes the *unpaid* domestic work that children, particularly girls, may do.[6] UK law draws yet further distinctions – 'employment' is any work 'for profit' by an employee. Moreover, babysitting – in terms of numbers, a significant children's job – is not considered 'employment' in terms of the current legislation. This lack of consistency has meant that statistics on the extent of children's work are hard to compare (see Chapter 1).

For the purposes of this book, the definition used is that of children's paid work. However, as many authors point out in their chapters, this does lead to important areas of children's lives being under represented.

The definition of child and children is also a significant issue. The UN Convention on the Rights of the Child defines children as up to the age of 18, the current voting age in the UK. However, the UK child employment laws apply in practice until the minimum school leaving age – the end of compulsory education which is 16 years. In many cases, those interviewed in this age group define themselves as 'young people' rather than as 'children'. The age range covered in this book is up to the minimum school leaving age, as other policies come into force in the UK at this stage. However, it is important to make links between children's work at school age and the transition into the world of work outside this age group. Although the majority of the chapters in this book are referring to children of the same age group, different terms have been used. In some cases they are referred to as young people, in others as children.

OUTLINE OF THE BOOK

The starting point of this book is an outline of what we know about the extent of children working in the UK. In Chapter 1, Sandy Hobbs and Jim McKechnie detail the proportion of children that work, the hours they do and the types of work which are undertaken. This chapter highlights the lack of a systematic collection of statistics which makes it hard to assess the exact numbers of children working. The chapter also outlines the gaps in the information on this issue in the UK, particularly related to children and young people from minority ethnic groups, and data from Northern Ireland.

In Chapter 2, Michael Lavalette gives a detailed analysis of the origins and evolution of children's work and of legislation in the UK. It traces the development of children's work through the industrial revolution, and the decline of children's work in the second half of the nineteenth century, to the growth of 'out-of-school work' which has set the pattern for children's work and its legislation today.

Sue Middleton, Jules Shropshire and Nicola Croden in Chapter 3 provide an analysis of family spending and children's work to explore the relationships between family poverty and children working. Their survey gives a detailed description of expenditure on children and their contributions to household income, focusing on families on income support and lone parent families. Although children in wealthier families are more likely to work, when children from families on income support or in lone parent families do work, they work longer hours for lower rates of pay, and on average earn more than children from richer families. The survey finds that working children are making a significant contribution to their families' living standards, contributing 2 per cent of total family income and 6 per cent in families on income support. Working children spend more on themselves and parents spend less on them than on non-working children.

Chapter 4 from Save the Children attempts to address the lack of children's voices in the debate around working children. It reports the results of qualitative research with children in the UK – both those who work and those who do not – about their attitudes towards children's employment. It focuses on the reasons for working, their experiences of work (both good and bad), how they are treated in the workplace, how they fit work into their lives and what they think of the current regulatory framework. The majority of the chapter is made up of direct quotes from children. Work plays a key part in their lives: the money is a way of gaining independence, socialising, and buying clothes and leisure equipment. As the research reported in Chapters 3 and 5 also found, some young people were contributing directly and indirectly to their household income.

In Chapter 5, Madeleine Leonard addresses the issue of children working in the context of poverty. It is a case study of a low income Catholic estate in West Belfast featuring high adult unemployment, an informal economy, with very low wage rates and high dependency on benefits. The children here who worked were working for extremely low rates of pay and some were working long hours. The majority did not contribute directly to household income – however, some did. Fewer children who worked received pocket money from their parents than those who did not work and most spent their earnings on clothing and leisure needs. Children were often employed informally by members of their wider kinship – often defined as 'helping out' – and played a key role in the informal economy. This chapter raises the issue of how to improve the situation of young workers in the context of poverty and an informal economy.

In Chapter 6, Ellen Heptinstall outlines the debate on whether work is healthy or harmful to children. This chapter focuses on accidents at work and reviews the literature on the psychological and educational effects of work on young people. Although there is serious under-reporting of accidents, evidence suggests that one in three children who work have suffered some form of accident; a further third of these have been so serious as to need medical attention. Young workers may be at greater risk of sustaining accidents at work – due to inexperience, different attitudes to risk-taking, and the specific nature of young workers' employment. Beyond accidents, the chapter looks at the positive and negative impact of working on school-age children, both in terms of providing work experience and the effect on education.

Chapter 7 follows on with further analysis of the debate on whether work is a positive experience for children. Norman Barton and Shirley Horton provide a case study of work experience in their school, while Jim McKechnie, Sandy Hobbs and Sandra Lindsay explore the relationship between education and children working, and the possibility of linking the two together. The study looks at the career paths of school children's work, and the potential contradiction between the positive elements of work placements in the school curriculum and the 'educational' aspects to children's work.

Chapter 8 by Rachel Marcus, Save the Children, analyses some of the lessons that can be learned from the debate about children and work in the international arena. Focusing on positive approaches, she analyses working children's involvement in addressing work-related problems. She identifies areas where this has had positive results in some overseas contexts and looks for lessons which could be applied in the UK.

In the last chapter, Ben Whitney brings an Education Welfare Officer's perspective to the debate. Grounded in the reality of regulating children who work in his area, he outlines the problems created by current anomalies in the law. He makes several proposals for changing the way in which children's work is viewed and regulated, including: national debate around why children work; making the procedure more meaningful by registering employers rather than children; and creating better links between school work and employment.

Finally, the Conclusion draws together the issues raised in preceding chapters. It makes recommendations for improving the situation of those children and young people who, whether through choice or force of circumstance, are working in the UK.

NOTES

1 For example, the Low Pay Unit and trade unions.
2 Although this aspect of children's work has received the greatest attention, it constitutes approximately 5 per cent of the work that children do worldwide.
3 A James and A Prout (eds), *Constructing and Reconstructing Childhood*, Falmer Press, 1990.
4 Some interesting studies do exist, for example M Song, '"Helping Out": Children's labour participation in Chinese take-away businesses in Britain' in J Brannen and M O'Brien, *Children in Families: Research and Policy*, Falmer Press, 1996.
5 See, for example, J Aldridge and S Becker, *Children who care, inside the world of young carers*, Loughborough Young Carers Research Group, Loughborough, 1993; C Dearden and S Becker, *Young Carers: The Facts*, Sutton Surrey, Read Business Publishing, 1995.
6 V Morrow, 'Responsible Children? Aspects of children's work and employment outside school in contemporary UK' in B Mayall, *Children's Childhoods: observed and experienced*, Falmer Press, 1994.

Children and work in the UK: the evidence

Sandy Hobbs and Jim McKechnie

In 1995, the official government publication, *Employment Gazette*, published the results of a survey of young people at work, carried out by the Economics, Research and Education Division of the Department of Employment.[1] By 'young people' the investigators meant those aged between 13 and 18 years. They found that just over half of those aged 13 to 15 worked at some time in the course of a year. Although this research has some limitations, it serves as a useful starting point for a discussion of the extent and nature of work by children in the UK today.

However, before considering what this research shows us, what it fails to show, and how it relates to information available from other sources, it is worth attempting to place this particular investigation in context. The period when it was conducted (1992) and when it was published (1995) was a time when the issue of child labour in Britain was achieving a higher political profile than it had had for some time. Angelika Hibbett and Mark Beatson, the authors of the report, state that their survey was the first 'comprehensive, nation-wide survey' of work by teenagers 'for over 20 years'. They do not describe what the earlier study had found or what followed its publication. They were presumably referring to *Work out of school*, a report of a study financed by the then Department of Health and Social Security and carried out by Emrys Davies.[2] Davies found that substantial numbers of children of school age were working. He also found that work appeared to have a detrimental effect on attitudes to education and performance at school. The report appeared in November 1972. In May 1973, the Employment of Children Act received the Royal Assent. In debate, it was made clear that Davis's findings had played a significant role in the then Conservative government's decision to support the Bill and facilitate its passage. To date this Act has still not been enforced.

For a time after the passage of the 1973 Act, child employment ceased to be a prominent political issue. Public discussion of it in the late 1970s and throughout the 1980s was limited. This cannot be explained by a decline in the extent of child labour. No further government sponsored studies appeared which could have justified such a claim. Smaller scale studies carried out by the London Low Pay Unit[3] suggested child employment was at quite a substantial level, at least in London and the South East of England, where the research was carried out.

With the 1990s came a change. This was partly due to a trickle of studies suggesting child employment was common in other parts of the country such as the West Midlands,[4] and Strathclyde.[5] These studies, undertaken by the London and Scottish Low Pay Units respectively, were treated with some disdain by government ministers. For example, Michael Forsyth, then a Minister at the Department of Employment, at a meeting of a House of Commons committee, challenged Pond and Searle's estimate that there might be up to 2 million children working in Britain.[6] The Low Pay Units and other pressure groups interested in the issue seemed to have a hard struggle to establish that there was any problem. And if no problem was acknowledged to exist, clearly no action would need to be undertaken.

However, another force was at work. The European Community had interested itself in child employment, culminating in the EU Council Directive on the Protection of Young People at Work passed in 1994 and due to be enacted in 1996. To the surprise of many, who saw the directive as moderate in its requirements and allowing many exemptions from its basic rules, the British government, unique among member nations, negotiated a four year delay in the implementation of some clauses.

It is against this background that the survey report by Hibbett and Beatson should be seen. In discussing the results of their Young People at Work survey, we shall keep in mind both the claims by pressure groups that child labour constitutes a problem in Britain today and the contrasting position of the government of the day that there was no evidence of any such problem.

HOW MANY CHILDREN WORK?

The obvious point with which to start is the evidence of the extent of work by children. This requires us to decide whom we are to treat as children. Hibbett and Beatson employed the term 'young people'. At the lower end of the scale, they include 13-year-olds, whom most people would probably agree are children, but at the other end of the scale are 18-year-olds, whom few would consider children. The most convenient place to draw the line is between 15 and 16, since compulsory education in Britain extends to the age of 16. It makes sense to distinguish between work by those subject to compulsory schooling and work by those beyond the minimum school leaving age.

The survey was conducted by interview and covered a representative sample of 1,663 13 to 18-year-olds throughout the United Kingdom. Within the sample there were 772 falling into the age range 13 to 15 years. They were asked whether they had worked at some time in the preceding year. Hibbett and Beatson found that for 13, 14 and 15-year-olds the proportions who had worked were 42 per cent, 51 per cent and 61 per cent respectively. Most of those working had had a single job, but some had had two or more. Males were more likely to have worked than females, but the percentage gap lessened as they got older. Hibbett and Beatson claimed that since their sample had been selected to be representative, it provided a sounder basis for estimating the extent of employment than other more limited studies. However, there appears not to be a big difference between their findings and those other studies which were reviewed by Hobbs, Lindsay and McKechnie in 1996.[7]

Unfortunately, direct comparisons between studies is difficult because different questions were asked. Various investigators have used different notions of what constitutes 'work', a point to which we shall return later. Sometimes information is collected on whether people are currently working, or have worked in the current school term, or have ever worked. Hibbett and Beatson focused on the year leading up to when the survey took place. Since, as we shall see, there is clear evidence that some children move in and out of jobs, we cannot use Hibbett and Beatson's findings as a good indicator of how many children have ever had work. The extent of child employment is also underestimated in their study by the fact that they do not look below the age of 13. This may have been because, with a few exceptions, work by children under 13 is forbidden by law. However, as we shall see shortly, the laws on child employment are widely ignored in Britain. In their review of other studies already mentioned, Hobbs, Lindsay and McKechnie[8] tentatively conclude that around 30 per cent of 12-year-olds and around 20 per cent of 11-year-olds have jobs. A subsequent MORI poll for the TUC produced similar results.[9] This would fit neatly with Hibbett and Beatson's percentages for the 13 to 15 year range, suggesting as it does a roughly 10 per cent increase in working year by year. If we supplement Hibbett and Beatson's results with other findings, one would conclude that a majority of children have been in employment by the time that they reach the minimum school leaving age.

Although they themselves do not publish the calculation, it is easy to derive from Hibbett and Beatson's figures an estimate of the child labour force in Britain. This can be done by using, on the one hand, their estimated national population of the 13 to 15 age group and, on the other hand, the percentages of 13, 14 and 15-year-olds in their sample who have worked in the past year. The outcome is a figure of just over 1.0 million. This is a good deal lower than Pond and Searle's estimate (1.75 to 2.0 million).[10] However, as we have already pointed out, Hibbett and Beatson do not include 11 and 12-year-olds, of whom we believe around 20 per cent and 30 per cent have jobs. Given that there are around 1.5 million children of this age in Britain, one could estimate that around 350,000 to 400,000 of them might have a job. Adding them to Hibbett and Beatson's figure, we find an estimate of 1.4 million 11 to 15-year-olds work. The Low Pay Unit estimate was not so misleading after all. The then government's rejection of their figures may have been based on honest doubts about the research methods employed by Pond and Searle, but research from a government department has shown that the scale of employment is roughly what these authors were claiming.

Hobbs, Lindsay and McKechnie[11] noted that a number of studies of older children found that many who were not working when questioned had nevertheless had jobs in the past. This category of 'former workers' needs to be taken into account when estimating the total number of children who will have had a job at some time during compulsory schooling. These authors put the figure at well over 2 million. A phenomenon of this scale surely demands attention.

Before leaving the question of how widespread child employment is, a word should be said about one aspect of the methods employed in the various studies cited. None of them were likely to throw up cases of children who have completely dropped out of school, or where they have become engaged in the more extreme and least tolerable types of work, such as prostitution. Evidence of child prostitution in Britain is unfortunately not difficult to come by, although to estimate its extent numerically is difficult.[12]

In addition, few child labour studies have taken ethnicity into account. Research in Greenwich, Blackburn and Birmingham suggests that Black and Asian children are less likely to be involved in paid employment outside of the family.[13] However, there are problems with sample sizes, and with the intepretation of the data.[14]

WHAT JOBS DO CHILDREN DO?

One way in which the importance of children working may be played down is by suggesting that they do only light, untaxing jobs. Unfortunately, the way in which Hibbett and Beatson classify the jobs undertaken is based on categories which may be meaningful for adult occupations but not for those aged 15 or less. Looking at industries, they found that in only two of the 10 categories were children found in any significant numbers. Distribution, hotels and catering and repairs as a group accounted for 71 per cent, while 'other services' accounted for 21 per cent. When the jobs were analysed in terms of occupational classes, 15 per cent of those working were found to be in sales occupations, 6 per cent in personal and protective services and 3 per cent in craft and related occupations. The large residue of 73 per cent was rather unhelpfully to be found in the category 'other occupations'. Clearly one must look elsewhere for a more informative breakdown of what jobs children are actually doing.

In collaboration with our colleagues, Sandra Lindsay and Michael Lavalette, we have carried out surveys of child employment in two areas of Scotland, one urban, one rural, and three areas of England – Blackburn, Cumbria and North Tyneside.[15]

Overall, the dominant category of employment is delivery work, including newspaper delivery, morning and evening, and milk delivery. It makes up as much as 40 per cent of the jobs in urban Scotland but only around a quarter of jobs in other areas. Children are employed in a wide range of other activities, including shop work (37 per cent in urban Scotland), hotel and catering (20 per cent in Cumbria) and waiting (17 per cent in rural Scotland). Somewhat smaller percentages of children were working in door to door selling, and in a range of jobs including packing, gardening, work in garages and building sites, cleaning, modelling and working in a sawmill.

It is necessary to keep in mind that the results obtained in such investigations may be influenced by the approach adopted. Babysitting and farm work illustrate this point. We found a substantial number of children were employed in babysitting (38 per cent in North Tyneside, 27 per cent in Blackburn, but a good deal fewer elsewhere). Some researchers such as Pond and Searle,[16] excluded babysitting from consideration, arguing that it is not prohibited by any legislation. However, since it is a common form of female employment, involves a payment and a degree of responsibility, we have included it.

In each area the percentage we found engaged in farm work is very low. The highest figure (only 4 per cent) was recorded in the rural Scottish area. However, this may in part be due to the fact that we excluded from consideration work within the family. We have no evidence of how many children work on their own family's farm. Our definition of 'work' may underestimate the extent of children working not only on farms but also in other family enterprises such as shops. In Blackburn, at the request of the local authority sponsoring the research, we included questions about paid work at home and paid work for the family outside the home. Around 16 per cent of pupils had done paid work at home. Rather more (26 per cent) said they had undertaken paid work outside the home for their parents. This compares with the finding of Hibbett and Beatson that 6 per cent of 13 to 15-year-olds who had not had any paid work outside the family had had paid work within the family in the year leading up to the survey. We feel such figures should be treated with caution. The relationship of work in the home, work in the family business, pocket money and payment is probably complex and difficult to explain to outsiders in the form of answers to a questionnaire.

A number of studies[17] have all produced data on the types of jobs being done by children in different parts of the country – including Birmingham, Coventry, Strathclyde and Greenwich. In each case, delivery work was the biggest single category, making up between 29 per cent and 54 per cent of jobs reported. Shop work and hotel and catering are also common, as is babysitting in those studies which included it. The MORI survey covering England and Wales found babysitting and delivery the most common jobs.[18]

The diversity of tasks carried out by children can be illustrated by the fact that the category 'Other' is often heavily used. It includes working in garages, on street markets, as furniture removers, on building sites, as cleaners, modelling and acting. Thus our results on the types of work carried out by children is not atypical. Children are employed in a wide variety of jobs, not all of which could be described as 'light'.

WHAT HOURS DO CHILDREN WORK?

One factor influencing how 'heavy' or 'light' work is, is the number of hours worked. Hibbett and Beatson found that 51 per cent of their 13 to 15-year-old sample worked up to five hours per week, 33 per cent worked between six and 12 hours, 16 per cent over 12 hours. We should remember in interpreting any evidence that school pupils spend on average 28 hours per week at school. The more time spent at work the less is left for leisure interests and homework. We find figures for hours per week averaging around eight hours a week. Approximately a fifth of those working were committing in excess of ten hours per week to their part-time employment.

TABLE 1.1: **Hours worked per week (percentages)**

	Up to 5	6 to 10	Over 10
Urban Scottish	48	31	21
Dumfries and Galloway	31	46	24
Cumbria	42	38	17
North Tyneside	36	41	22
Blackburn	46	37	16

Source: Hobbs and McKechnie, 1997.

This pattern was fairly consistent across the regions, percentages varying only between 16 and 24. It should be noted too that in a few cases children reported working a great deal more than 10 hours per week. There is a possibility that longer working hours may have a detrimental effect on school performance. For a discussion of this issue, see Hobbs and McKechnie,[19] and Chapters 6 and 7 of this book.

Comparing our results with findings from other studies is problematic due to the variations in the categories used. MacLennan, Fitz and Sullivan noted that in their early 1980s study the majority of children worked for 10 hours or less per week.[20] However, they found that a large minority did work in excess of 11 hours per week. Mizen found that the average number of hours worked per week in his sample was seven hours, with 29 per cent working more than eight hours per week.[21] Lavalette found around a quarter of his sample worked 10 hours per week or more.[22] Balding's 14 to 15-year-old sample is the most comparable to Lavalette's and he found 16 per cent of them working as much as that.[23] The TUC survey found that 29 per cent of those with summer jobs worked over 10 hours per week.[24]

The comparison of the various studies suggests some degree of consistency in their findings. There is a large enough percentage of children working in excess of 10 hours per week to warrant concern, particularly when we bear in mind that these are full-time school students. The more hours a child works, the fewer are available for family, friends, leisure and homework.

We also considered the time of day when these hours are worked. The amended Children and Young Persons Act 1933, and the equivalent 1937 Act for Scotland, specify that children are prohibited from working before 7am and after 7pm. In each area which was studied, many children had started work before 7am (43 per cent in Blackburn being the highest). Working after 7pm is even more common, ranging from 42 per cent in Blackburn to 63 per cent in rural Scotland.

Of course, stopping and starting times reported do not usually refer to the same job. They should be taken as indicating when in the day a particular job is undertaken. The most obvious 'time-linked' activities are milk and newspaper delivery. The former is almost always an early morning task.

Few other studies provide much information on starting and finishing times. Pond and Searle note some of the pupils in their studies worked at illegal times but they did not specify the numbers.[25] Lavalette found that a large percentage were working before 7am (ranging from 23 per cent to 44 per cent). Similarly, a large percentage of pupils were working beyond the 7pm watershed (ranging from 40 per cent to 69 per cent). The Trades Union Congress survey found that 36 per cent of children had worked before 7am and 53 per cent had worked after 7pm.[26]

HOW MUCH DO CHILDREN EARN?

Some people assume that child employment is undertaken for 'pocket money'. Others assume that children work at least in part because of their family's poverty. Yet another view is that children feel the need to work to fulfil the 'needs' created by a consumer society. Whichever view is correct, and they may all contain some element of truth, it is worth trying to establish just how much children actually earn.

This was an aspect of child employment not covered by Hibbett and Beatson's study.[27] In our investigations, average hourly rates of pay ranged from £1.79 to £2.34. Weekly pay ranged from an average of £11.85 to £13.80. Mizen found the average hourly and weekly rates of pay were £1.60 and £13.70, respectively.[28] Balding provides a breakdown of weekly earnings and, since he also provides the average hours worked, it is possible to calculate the hourly rate of pay for his sample.[29] Averages are broadly similar to other studies. For both males and females, there is a general tendency for rates to rise with age, except for an unexpected dip in rates at age 12-13.

TABLE 1.2: **Hourly earnings (averages)**

	per hour	per week
Urban Scottish	£2.34	£13.97
Dumfries and Galloway	£1.79	£12.99
Cumbria	£2.11	£13.80
North Tyneside	£1.80	£11.85

Source: Hobbs and McKechnie, 1997.

Jolliffe et al found that 45 per cent of working children were earning less than £10.00 per week and that 78 per cent earned less than £20.00 per week.[30] Pond and Searle found that the average hourly rate of pay was £1.80.[31] The majority of the employed children (52 per cent) were earning £2.00 or less per hour. In addition, they remind us of the dangers of dealing with 'average' income, namely that it can conceal the marked variation that can exist around the mean value. They report that a small percentage (7 per cent) of the children in their sample were earning 50 pence or less an hour. At the other extreme they found one instance of a child earning £8.33 per hour. We have also found this wide variation in pay rates in our research. The lowest hourly pay rate we recorded was 10 pence per hour. The Trades Union Congress did not report average weekly earnings but for both term-time and summer holiday jobs, the median wage fell in the £10 to £19 band.[32]

DO CHILDREN WORK ILLEGALLY?

Legislation on child employment requires local authorities to create byelaws and enforce them. All of the authorities in the areas we studied had opted for a permit system. Thus, any child found working in any of our studies should have a valid permit. Hibbett and Beatson did not examine this issue.

According to our findings, to have a work permit is rare. In four areas the number of current and former workers who had ever had a permit ranged from 1 per cent in urban Scotland to 7 per cent in North Tyneside. In only one area, rural Scotland, had substantially higher proportions of child workers had permits. There the average was 29 per cent. In one school in that area, about half of the working pupils had permits. However, the other schools in the area also had higher than average permit rates. Further investigation of the schools showed that they all placed a deliberate emphasis on providing information about the permit system to their pupils. The school with the highest permit rate was the most rigorous in pursuing this policy. The high permit rate therefore probably reflects this proactive stance.

Another important issue in a review of the legal status of child employment is age. The data we collected focused on pupils of 14 and 15 years of age. As such our respondents were above the legal minimum age. We asked participants to provide us with information on their age when they first entered paid employment outside of the family. From their replies, it is evident that a number of children start work below 13, the legal minimum age. Typically, between a fifth and a third of all pupils with experience of paid employment say they started work before they were legally eligible to do so.

In Blackburn, children in the first year of secondary school were included in the sample. These pupils will normally be about 12 years of age. While fewer pupils in the first year were working than in later years, 20 per cent were currently working and a further 8 per cent were former workers. Balding's data also indicated that children are employed in 'regular paid work' in the first year of secondary schooling.[33]

The final issue to mention with respect to legality are the types of jobs done by children. We have already discussed the problems involved in researching this area. These can increase if we are attempting to decide whether any given job falls inside or outside the law. An example may clarify this. In the area of work generally described as hotel and catering work, delivering food to a table would fall within the law, while working in the kitchen would not. A further difficulty arises from the existence of local authority byelaws which vary in what jobs they prohibit. Nevertheless, it can still be said that there is evidence that children find themselves working in prohibited areas. A number of the jobs which we placed in the 'other' category when outlining the variations in children's jobs previously are clearly illegal. Examples of children working in a sawmill, as a garage mechanic and working on a fishing boat were found. It is also evident from the descriptions given by children of their work that many are working in environments which are prohibited, for example, working in the preparation of food.

The extent of work without permits or breaking some restriction which we have found is confirmed by other studies. MacLennan et al estimate that in their study four out of five children were working illegally.[34] Jolliffe et al adopt a similar approach and conclude that 88 per cent of the children working in their sample were employed illegally since they broke one or other of the regulations.[35] Similarly, Pond and Searle express concern about the illegal nature of much of child employment.[36] In their study they estimate 74 per cent were working illegally, 33 per cent involved in jobs that were prohibited.

ARE THERE RISKS TO HEALTH AND SAFETY?

Hibbett and Beatson provide no information on accidents to children at work.[37] However, data from the Health and Safety Commission indicates that the level of accidents to working children is low, bearing in mind the numbers of children working – one fatal accident per year, with non-fatal accidents typically around 35.[38] However, a number of suggestions can be made to explain this. The Commission acknowledges that under-reporting of accidents occurs. Furthermore, since most under 16-year-olds are employed illegally, there may be a desire not to report accidents. In addition, the Commission figures focus upon specific categories of accident, notably fatalities or accidents that involve absence from work for more than three days. While relatively few children may be involved in accidents which fall into these categories, accidents which are treated as relatively minor in adults may have greater significance in childhood or adolescence.

In the research by MacLennan, Fitz and Sullivan, Pond and Searle, and Jolliffe and others, 31 per cent, 35 per cent and 36 per cent of child workers respectively reported having had an accident at work.[39] In our studies, the figures are somewhat lower, ranging from 17 per cent (urban Scotland) to 23 per cent (North Tyneside). These figures are similar to the 19 per cent of child workers reporting having had an accident in the survey for the Trades Union Congress.[40] This may be because we included children not currently working, but who had worked in the past. Some of them may have forgotten about an accident. Another fact may be the types of jobs included. For example, if babysitting is a form of employment where accidental injury is rare, it will have the effect of reducing the overall percentage of accidents recorded in studies which include it within their definition of employment.

We recently undertook a small scale study at three schools in Scotland.[41] Reported levels of accidents were similar to those found in our previous studies (ranging from 17 per cent in one school to 22 per cent in another). The main purpose of the study was to explore any possible links between accidents and type of job undertaken.

The majority of accidents (62 per cent) occur in delivery work, a form of employment which is widely perceived as acceptable 'children's work'. The next highest number of accidents (16 per cent) was reported in the 'other' category. This includes such jobs as cleaner, care worker, and working on clay pigeon shooting range. Predominantly, these are jobs from which children are supposedly excluded by law. The types of accidents reported included some which may be included in the Health and Safety Commission categories, such as a broken arm, broken foot and fractured fingers. In addition, a range of lesser accidents were reported, including burns and cuts, none of which would have been included and would therefore not be officially recorded. However, they cannot be regarded as insignificant.

CONCLUSION

Enough research on child employment in Britain has now been published to allow us to answer certain basic questions with confidence. Many children work. The types of jobs they do vary considerably. Legal restrictions are not enforced. All these points seem clear. However, more research is needed to answer other questions. We have little detailed information about what school-aged workers actually do in their jobs. Do they learn? Are they bored? Are they in danger? We do not know enough about those children who work in the most extreme jobs such as prostitution. More needs to be done to examine the relationship between employment and the rest of the young worker's life. How do they spend their earnings? Do jobs affect relationships within the family? How do jobs affect schooling? All these questions are worth posing, particularly now that we can be sure that having a part-time job is common among children in the UK.

NOTES

1 A Hibbett and M Beatson, 'Young people at work', *Employment Gazette*, 103, 1995, pp169-177.
2 E Davies, 'Work out of school', *Education*, 10 November 1972, pp i-iv.
3 E MacLennan, J Fitz and J Sullivan, *Working Children*, Low Pay Unit, 1985.
4 C Pond and A Searle, *The Hidden Army: Children at work in the 1990s*, Low Pay Unit, 1991.
5 M Lavalette, J McKechnie and S Hobbs, *The Forgotten Workforce: Scottish children at work*, Scottish Low Pay Unit, 1991.
6 House of Commons European Standing Committee B, *Protection of young people at work*, HMSO, 1993.
7 S Hobbs, S Lindsay and J McKechnie, 'The extent of child employment in Britain', *British Journal of Education and Work*, 9, 1996, pp5-18.
8 *Ibid.*
9 Trades Union Congress, *Working Classes: a TUC report on school age labour in England and Wales*, TUC, 1997.
10 Pond and Searle, *op cit*.
11 Hobbs, Lindsay and McKechnie, *op cit*.
12 See, for example, M Lee and R O'Brien, *Redefining child prostitution*, Children's Society, 1995.

13 F Jolliffe, S Patel, Y Sparks and K Reardon, *Child Employment in Greenwich*, London Borough of Greenwich, Education Social Work Service; Pond and Searle, *op cit*; M Lavalette, S Lindsay, S Hobbs and J McKechnie, *Child Employment in Blackburn, a report to Blackburn Borough Council*, Universities of Liverpool and Paisley, 1996.

14 S Hobbs and J McKechnie, *Child Employment in Britain: a social and psychological analysis*, Stationery Office, 1997.

15 Our main findings are outlined in *ibid*.

16 Pond and Searle, *op cit*.

17 Pond and Searle, *op cit*; P Mizen, 'Learning the hard way: The extent and significance of child working in Britain', *British Journal of Education and Work*, 5, 1992, pp5–17; J Balding, *Young people in 1992*, Schools Health Education Unit, School of Education, University of Exeter, 1993; M Lavalette, *Child employment in the capitalist labour market*, Avebury, 1994; Jolliffe *et al*, *op cit*.

18 TUC, *op cit*.

19 Hobbs and McKechnie, *op cit*.

20 MacLennan *et al*, *op cit*.

21 Mizen, *op cit*.

22 Lavalette, *op cit*.

23 Balding, *op cit*.

24 TUC, *op cit*.

25 Pond and Searle, *op cit*.

26 Lavalette, *op cit*; TUC, *op cit*.

27 Hibbert and Beatson, *op cit*.

28 Mizen, *op cit*.

29 Balding, *op cit*.

30 Jolliffe *et al*, *op cit*.

31 Pond and Searle, *op cit*.

32 TUC, *op cit*.

33 Balding, *op cit*.

34 MacLennan *et al*, *op cit*.

35 Jolliffe *et al*, *op cit*.

36 Pond and Searle, *op cit*.

37 Hibbert and Beatson, *op cit*.

38 Health and Safety Commission, *Health & Safety Statistics 1994-5*, Health and Safety Executive, 1996.

39 MacLennan *et al*, *op cit*; Pond and Searle, *op cit*; Jolliffe *et al*, *op cit*.

40 TUC, *op cit*.

41 J McKechnie, S Hobbs, S Lindsay and M Lynch, 'Working children: the health and safety issue', *Children and Society*, 12, 1998, pp38–47.

2

Child labour: historical, legislative and policy context

Michael Lavalette

It is often said that children have always worked. This is almost certainly true. However, such claims can lead us to oversimplify; to amalgamate a series of experiences of child work that are quite different and to ignore the range of contexts within which that activity takes place. This chapter offers a historical review, noting both continuities and changes in the nature of child labour in Britain.

A significant historical debate about child work and the growth of modern society is between two groups, 'optimists' and 'pessimists', and concerns the social consequences of the industrial revolution. Optimists like, for example, Ivy Pinchbeck argue that the worst examples of child labour exploitation occurred in the cottage industries during the period of 'proto-industrialisation'. Here parents, and fathers in particular, forced their children to work long hours in terrible conditions, with children treated as disposable family possessions. The industrial revolution brought production out of the home into the public sphere and, initially, similar work practices occurred.[1]

Crucially, however, the visibility of child labour in this period provoked government action and the plight of such child workers produced a progressive legislative programme, instigated by the British political establishment, which recognised that child labour was immoral and grossly exploitative.[2]

On the other hand, pessimists, like the historian E P Thompson, argue that the excesses of child labour exploitation during the first half of the nineteenth century 'was one of the most shameful events in our history'.[3]

I will deal with this debate in the following two sections but its importance is not merely historical. It leads us to look at the role of state legislation in attempts to control child labour, to look in detail at what sections of working class children were employed in the most exploitative forms of child labour and, finally, to consider whether the removal of children from the main sectors of the labour market in the last quarter of the nineteenth century was beneficial to the children themselves or whether it resulted in working class children being locked into a set of increasingly oppressive institutions and experiences associated with modern childhood. These are themes which will reappear throughout this book.

CHILD LABOUR DURING 'PROTO-INDUSTRIALISATION'

The term 'proto-industrialisation' has been criticised by some historians for being 'vague', but, according to Levine,[4] it allows us to identify the growth and increasing influence of an integrated market system in the 100 years prior to the 'take-off' of the industrial revolution in Britain (circa 1780). This period saw the development of more complex trading patterns and arrangements and the increasing privatisation of the means of production in the hands of capitalists and merchants, who also increased their control over access to the market. The labour process, however, by and large remained under the control of the direct producer.

In this period production was organised in many different ways. There were, however, two dominant models. The first was where the household functioned as a self-contained unit, differentiated internally so that each member had a specific task in the production of a complete commodity. An example of this was textile manufacturing in which different members of the weaver's family carded wool, spun the yarn and wove the cloth. The second method involved differentiation between households specialising in particular tasks, be it combing, spinning or weaving. Here the article was passed by the merchant or an agent from one stage in production to the next.[5] As production outpaced the needs of local consumption the middlemen and traders played an increasingly important role in transporting the commodity to the point of sale. As Levine notes, although the merchants did not directly supervise the process of production, they 'exerted power over the myriad of rural workers by controlling their access to the markets in which their goods were sold. Because the merchant capitalist controlled the market place he was able to force down wages'.[6]

The interesting point to assess is the extent to which these features increased the exploitation of child labour. The market increasingly forced a logic onto the entire production process. For the craft worker in her/his domestic setting there was a need increasingly to employ the cheapest units of labour power available. Two specific points must be recognised at this juncture. First, increasing specialisation and technological advance had had the effect of deskilling and cheapening labour. Second, the cheapest labour available was that provided by women and children from within the family or alternatively from 'apprenticed' child labour. These two elements were mutually reinforcing and, as a result, it became increasingly difficult for any family to survive on one wage alone.

In other words, there was an interaction of social, economic and technological features which affected the general position of child labourers at this period. The plight of child workers within the domestic industries was exceptionally harsh. From weaving, spinning and lace making to straw plaiting and button making, the evidence gathered by Pinchbeck shows a horrendous level of child exploitation.[7] The children's hours were often long, the tasks quite specialised and repetitive, the conditions very often cramped, dank and generally unhealthy and the employer, journeyman or parents, often brutal in their extraction of labour from the child.

An important source for historians of child labour in proto-industrial Britain is Daniel Defoe's *Tour Through The Whole Island of Great Britain* (1724).[8] However, the frequent use of this source leaves one major questioned unanswered: if the use of children's labour during the proto-industrial period was as common as has so far been suggested, then why was it viewed as noteworthy, and not simply the norm, by Defoe? This question suggests that the overall picture was more complex. Clearly, children could be found labouring in excessively exploitative conditions for long hours within cottage industries. Yet, it would seem that overall there were fewer opportunities for children to work than has often been assumed.

This, in general terms, is the argument presented by Cunningham who suggests that employment outlets for children were limited and the actual tasks they performed were crucially shaped by the local employment structure.[9] Cunningham suggests that child under-employment and unemployment, more than child labour, was the social problem that commentators, theorists and politicians were concerned with during the eighteenth century. He also suggests that there was a chronological aspect to child employment. Although evidence can be gathered which shows very young children working in domestic industries, it is clear that children were more likely to find employment as they got older and physically became more able to complete an arduous day's labour. Cunningham's conclusions are forceful. They do not deny the existing evidence concerning the horrendous effects of labour activities performed by children. Nor do they idealise the plight of children who did not work but were a 'drain' on family resources. The life of the unemployed child was one of extreme hardship, want and starvation. The element that linked the hardship brought by child unemployment and child labour exploitation was the growth of the market and the imposition of market relations onto everyday life.

Thus, the exploitation of child labour became more intensive with the spread of competitive market relations and the commodification of labour. In the proto-industrial period, families were forced to work long hours, in terrible conditions, for little reward. To increase family income all family members, including very young children, were forced to work. There is little doubt that children were treated harshly under this system but the family's control over the production process, though not over access to the market, offered some potential respite. It was precisely the loss of control over the production process and the separation of home and work that ushered in the intensification of child labour exploitation that was witnessed in the factories, mills and mines during the industrial revolution.

CHILD LABOUR AND THE INDUSTRIAL REVOLUTION

Much of the difficulty in assessing the role played by children in the industrial revolution (*circa* 1780-1850) is related to the fact that the period was marked by uneven development, change and the imposition of new ideas and methods of production. As in domestic industry, child factory labour varied both geographically and by industry. This noted, the crucial difference separating this form of child labour exploitation from previous examples was the fact that in the burgeoning factories the children were utilised as individual workers, the pace and intensity of their labour determined by machines and regulated by overseers, with little account taken of their developmental needs as children.

There were two distinct phases in the employment of children in the factories. Initially, factories and mills faced a shortage of labour. This was partially due to their geographical location, near to running water and away from the main population centres, and partly reflected the attitude of many parents who were reluctant to send their children into factories and mills where they would be subject to the authority of others. In these circumstances, the system developed whereby parish apprentices were sent by Poor Law Guardians to provide the required workforce. Guardians in towns like London made agreements with employers in the north of England to take numbers of pauper children from the age of six upwards. Housed in specially built 'prentice houses' they were dependent on their employer for food and shelter. Their work hours were excessive, often lasting 15 hours a day. The *Report on Children in Manufactories* (1816), notes the example of one Lancashire mill which employed 150 pauper apprentices, whose hours were from 5am till 8pm, with only two half-hour breaks at 7am and 12 noon, for breakfast and lunch. However, in busy periods, or when time had to be made up, the finishing time was often extended until 9 or 10pm.[10]

The second phase occurred with the development of factory production in urban settings. This did not dramatically alter the working conditions of children, but it shifted the costs of maintaining and reproducing labour onto families (ie, families were now responsible for feeding, clothing and housing children). This increased the financial burdens on families so that, whenever the opportunity arose, all family members would enter the labour market. In other words, families were increasingly forced to utilise all the labour resources at their disposal to meet their subsistence needs. Hence, with industrialisation, the form, rate and intensity of the exploitation of child labour dramatically increased. Hammond and Hammond suggest that whereas previously child labour had in many ways been supplementary, in factory production it became essential to the production process. Thus they note that: 'under the early factory system the employment of the masses of children was the foundation of industry'.[11]

Making the problem of child labour potentially more problematic for working class families was the fact that the spread of factory production made it *possible*, in some sectors, for 'expensive' adult male labour to be substituted by 'cheaper' female and child labour. This was one *tendency* within the labour market at the time.[12] In some trades this may partially explain working class resistance to child labour. Substitutionism, the replacement of adult male labour by female and/or child labour, had an impact on the entire family, forcing men out of work and women and children into longer hours for less money, all to the benefit of the employers of labour. This, however, was only a trend in some employment sectors. Often children did not replace adult male workers because they were employed to perform distinct children's tasks, jobs which were identified as particularly appropriate for children. In other words, many children performed necessary, but subsidiary, tasks within the overall production process and adult men, women and children were non-competing sections of the workforce.[13]

These processes did not affect all children in the same way. There are two important issues to recognise. First, as Horrell and Humphries note, fatherless children and orphans were more likely to suffer most, to find themselves in the worst employment situations or forced into areas of work where there were labour shortfalls.[14] Thus it was among the most oppressed and downtrodden sections of the working class that child labour exploitation was at its most extreme. Secondly, the uneven development of industrial capitalism and local employment structures affected the amount and type of labour available to children in different geographical locations. This spatial aspect to child employment is important because it meant that in some areas, as during the proto-industrial period, there were few jobs for children to perform and there were always more children actively seeking work than there were jobs available.[15]

One peculiarity that developed out of the Factory Acts of 1833 and 1844 was the existence of 'half-time working' in textile factories. Children would spend most of their day at work and some in education. The 1833 Act prohibited children under nine from working in cotton, woollen, worsted, hemp, flaw, tow or linen mills or factories and stated that:

> no child between the ages of nine and thirteen should be employed without a schoolmaster's certificate showing that the child had attended school for at least 2 hours a day during the proceeding week.[16]

The Factory Act (1844) reduced the age children could start work from nine to eight, but their daily hours were cut from eight to six and a half. Finally, all children between the ages of eight and 13 employed in textile factories were required to attend school for three hours a day.

According to Frow and Frow, during the second half of the nineteenth century the main effects of the various Factory Acts, with regard to child labour and educational regulation, was to standardise the requirements of the 1844 Act to other employment sectors.[17] It was not until 1878 that factories were prohibited from employing children under the age of 10. Half-time working remained in place until 1918 when it was abolished by the Education Act of that year.

Generally, during the second half of the nineteenth century there was a marked decline in the level of child employment from the high point in the 1830s and 1840s.[18] We can plot this decline by looking at census returns from 1851 (Table 2.1).

TABLE 2.1 **Census data on child workers (1851-1911) (percentage working)**

	Year						
Gender/Age	1851	1861	1871	1881	1891	1901	1911
Boys 5-9	2.0	2.0	0.8	–	–	–	–
Girls 5-9	1.4	1.1	0.7	–	–	–	–
Boys 10-14	36.6	36.9	32.1	22.9	26.0	21.9	18.3
Girls 10-14	19.9	20.2	20.5	15.1	16.3	12.0	10.4

Source: H Cunningham and P P Viazzo (eds), Child Labour in Historical Perspective 1800-1995, Unicef, 1996

These figures plot the generally declining trend in child labour in the second half of the nineteenth century. The figures for 1861 and 1891 show an increase over the previous census suggesting that economic conditions will affect children's access to jobs as they do with other groups of workers. Indeed, Cunningham surmises that annual figures would more emphasise the fluctuating nature of child employment and its link with economic conditions.[19] The figures themselves are inadequate because they omit many children working in the informal sector or in illegal employment, do not include the work performed by girls (mainly) in and around the home or rearing siblings and hide spatial variation in children's employment rates. Nevertheless, the figures do indicate a decline in child labour. After 1881 children between the ages of five and nine are not recorded because their numbers are so small and there is evidence which indicates that in the 10 to 14 category it is 13 and 14-year-old children who are working by the turn of the century and not 10, 11 and 12-year-olds.[20] So the second half of the nineteenth century generally witnessed a decline in child labour and a raising of the age of child workers; young children had almost ceased working by the 1880s.

THE DECLINE OF CHILD LABOUR

Given the apparent fall in the numbers of children working in the second half of the nineteenth century, the obvious question to ask is why did this decline take place?

The reasons for the fall in the number of child workers have been hotly contested over recent years. A number of authors have attempted to explain the process by reference to changes in one or more areas of children's lives. For Nardinelli, the decline of child labour is a consequence of working class family strategy.[21] He suggests that rising living standards (and male occupational earnings in particular) allowed working class families to 'invest' in their children. By forgoing short-term financial reward, in the form of children's wages, families could invest in children's education, allowing them to accumulate human capital and obtain better jobs and rewards later in life.

Clearly, as Horrell and Humphries argue, rising family income did allow working class families to control, to some extent, the supply of labour onto the market.[22] But it is not clear that the motives were those identified by Nardinelli. Attempts to establish a family wage may have represented a strategy to increase family income but it was largely an unsuccessful one. In many areas, the imposed education system was often rejected as undue state interference in an activity that should be controlled by workers' mutual organisations. The claim that working class families perceived (and acted upon) a link between education, work and improved income needs to be proved. Finally, the unevenness in workers' wages does not neatly fit with child labour patterns (either chronologically or geographically). In other words, it is not the case that an increase in wages always resulted in a decline in child labour levels, and vice versa

For a number of writers, child labour declined as a consequence of state legislation and regulation of the labour market.[23] This, in essence, is the 'optimists' case. It is argued that the horrors of the factory system led to campaigners exerting pressure on government which, as a consequence, brought in a regulatory regime which effectively prohibited the employment of children in 'inappropriate' outlets. However, state regulation of child labour was brought in very unevenly throughout the nineteenth century. Legislation potentially posed a conflict between two pillars of nineteenth-century society. On the one hand, it involved state regulation of the labour market and therefore stood against the dominant *laissez-faire* orthodoxy of the time. Further, labour market activity was thought to be good for children, in as much as it instilled good habits of industry. On the other hand, regulating legitimate activities for children was part of the process of controlling working class children and imposing an 'acceptable' childhood onto the working class. This conflict took place between sections of the economic and political governing classes with some advocates of protectionism likening child labour to slavery (for example, Lord Shaftesbury), while others railed against the effects legislation would have on their competitive abilities.

Against this background, it is perhaps not surprising that child labour regulation developed in an often contradictory and confusing way. The consequence was that child labour law was only gradually introduced and the development of the legal framework for the control of child labour was never set out in any coherent manner. Generally the process was one where a rising tide of opposition to child labour in one sector of the economy would (eventually) be met with proposed legislation. Such proposals, however, would provoke opposition from groups claiming that legislation would have an impact on adult hours and wages, and on the price of British commodities vis-à-vis their international competitors. Such claims were often partially successful so that nominally restricting legislation would contain a number of potential loopholes and escape clauses.[24]

Any notion of an enlightened approach by the British establishment is clearly questioned by the example of the chimney sweepers. The plight of chimney sweepers is well known. Young children were sent up chimneys both to clean them and to fight fires in the flues. As Hammond and Hammond note, 'some flues which the children swept were only seven inches square. For such chimneys not only a tiny child but a naked tiny child was necessary.'[25] Chimney climbing did not take place in obscure far away cottages but in middle class homes in the towns and cities; their conditions of work were well known. Foreign competition could hardly be blamed for the need to continue this work practice. Yet despite various campaigns to control chimney climbers (originating in the 1760s), the first attempts at licensing were not brought in until The Chimney Sweepers Act (1875).

Nevertheless, by the end of the nineteenth century, regulation of child labour was accepted as a legitimate state activity and clearly had some impact on the child labour market. Finally, for Weiner[26] and Fyfe[27] the growth of compulsory education effectively stopped child labour because it required children to be at school during the main periods of work activity. Cunningham clearly recognises the importance of the growth of the schooling system but, for him, this has as much to do with solving the problem of child unemployment and under-employment in inner city locations.[28] The move to compulsory education (through the Education Acts 1870, 1880, 1918) was clearly a very important element affecting the number of children working. It increasingly identified an 'appropriate children's activity' that would be performed during the main part of the day. While there were a variety of reasons for the growth and expansion of the education system it gradually left working children with a choice: truancy and employment or education and working during out-of-school hours. Around the turn of the century children clearly followed both strategies. But, gradually, the combination of the increasing power of truancy officers (and various other welfare officials) over the lives of working class children and families, the moral pressure brought on (large) employers who continued to employ children, and changes to the employment structure meant that the majority of children occupied marginal jobs that could be combined with schooling.

Thus, to some extent, each of the above explanations offers a piece of the jigsaw that explains the changing form of child labour in Britain at the turn of the twentieth century. But each of these explanations is only partial and needs to be placed on a wider screen. They were part of a process of change which affected many areas of social, political and economic life at the end of the nineteenth century and which witnessed increasing state activity to structure social relations in a context of an increasingly internationalised competitive socio-economic system.[29] The 'marginalisation of child labour' (refer-ring to the dual process whereby children were removed from the main sectors of employment to the margins of the labour market where they in turn performed marginal economic tasks) occurred at a particular juncture in the development of British history. It is to the consequences of the marginalisation process for child workers that we now turn.

THE TRANSFORMATION OF CHILD LABOUR – GROWTH OF OUT-OF-SCHOOL WORK

In the period between 1880 and 1918, child labour was transformed into two separate problems: the question of 'out-of-school' work and the 'boy labour problem' in the developing youth labour market. The ability of children to gain work out of school reflected economic changes in the structure of employment that were taking place at the turn of the century. The development of 'organised capitalism' brought dramatic socio-economic changes in Britain.[30] Harris has identified this period as one of major 'structural change'.[31] It saw the development of electricity and telegraphic communications, new industries such as electrical engineering, steel shipbuilding and large scale chemical production. Yet such changes also brought poverty and unemployment associated with the break-up of the old industries and the growth of casual work in the 'unregulated' sectors of the economy.[32] One consequence of such changes in the employment structure was that jobs were increasingly being created, or existing jobs were being adapted, to allow children to combine the demands of both education and work. As the 1902 report of the governmental Inter-Departmental Committee states:

> their [ie, school children's] employment in … occupations outside the school hours is wholly unregulated. The result has been that, as the door has been closed to their employment in factories and workshops during school hours, there has been a tendency … towards their employment in other occupations before morning school, between school hours, in the evening and on Saturdays and Sundays.[33]

Partly as a consequence, the issue of children's out-of-school work received increasing attention from middle class philanthropists at the turn of the century. Not only was it felt to interfere with children's schooling but, equally, it was identified as subjecting young workers to undesirable contacts and experiences and would lead them into 'blind alley' employment on completing their schooling.

One of the initiators of such concern was Edith Hogg who, in 1897, published an article, 'School Children As Wage Earners' in the journal *Nineteenth Century*. This focused interest on the issue and was instrumental in pressurising the House of Commons to agree to obtain a 'Return of Elementary School Children Working For Wages' (1902). Forms were issued to 20,000 elementary schools in England and Wales and returns were obtained from all but 520. The Return provides interesting pointers to the change that was occurring in the form of child labour at this time. Some of the tasks the Return suggests the children had are given in Table 2.2 below.

TABLE 2.2 **Return of elementary school children working for wages**	
Type of job	
Selling newspapers (though not door-to-door delivery)	15,182
Hawking	2,435
Service in shops	76,173
Agriculture	6,115
Odd jobs	10,636
Minding babies	11,585
Other occasional tasks	8,627
House and laundry work	9,254
Needlework, cardbox marking etc	4,019
Total	**144,026**
Source: J E Gorst, *The Children of the Nation*, Methuen, 1907	

The return was incomplete and inadequate, yet, despite this, it showed 179,000 children worked for wages while attending school full time. No notice was to be taken of 'those in casual or seasonal employment', but it was precisely these jobs which allowed children to combine work and schooling. There was ambiguity concerning the definition of 'casual' jobs and this led to variation in school response. Yet the remarkable feature is that, with the exception of the last category listed in Table 2.2 above, the jobs listed closely match those which most surveys suggest children undertake today (see Chapter 1).

Out-of-school work was far from being easy or 'light' employment. Sherard notes a number of examples. His first concerns a young boy in Glasgow who, 'working in the morning for a milkman and in the evening for a grocer "put in" out of school hours an eight hour day of work'.[34] This example came from a study which suggested that over 4,000 school children in Glasgow were working in out-of-school employment. As Sherard claims, out-of-school work involves children 'in wage-earning labour, often of a dangerous, sometimes of a fatal, and almost always of an exhausting nature'.[35]

The Inter-Departmental Committee of 1902 went on record as deploring the long hours that children worked, especially when combined with required school hours, and the fact that much of children's labour activities went on without legal protection. Nevertheless, it suggested that 70 per cent of child workers were employed for less than 20 hours a week and hence, provided that children's employment was restricted to between 20 and 25 hours a week, it would not be harmful. Indeed, the Committee claimed, 'moderate work was in many cases not only not injurious but positively beneficial'.[36] (See also Chapter 1.)

Both Sherard and the Inter-Departmental Committee noted that many children throughout the country were performing the same types of jobs: running errands, selling newspapers, delivering milk, working in shops and street selling. These were consistently viewed as children's jobs. However, they also note that there were other jobs which were specific to particular areas. Hence, the work opportunities for children clearly varied depending on the needs of the local economy. Such a recognition was important as it is this feature above all that pushed the Committee to suggest that the best means of controlling the worst aspects of child labour was via the use of local authority byelaws, a practice which, in theory, continues to this day.

Thus, in the early part of the twentieth century, child labour was significant in two forms. First, children working full time, either legally or illegally, were still important. One possible solution to this problem was to reinforce school attendance legislation and to punish truancy. The difficulty the authorities faced in pursuing this aim, however, was that government legislation and local bye-laws still allowed half-time working and 'early leaving' for children who had reached a set standard or had a set number of school attendances in their preceding school careers. This meant that the school leaving age could, in reality, be quite flexible and based on an individual child's performance and/or attendance. These circumstances made 'truancy' detection harder and the legal requirements more difficult to implement. These problems were not solved until the Education Act (1918) which required all children to attend school full time until the age of 14.

Secondly, children's out-of-school labour was identified as problematic to the extent that it interfered with their education (through excessive hours) or encouraged them to take full-time jobs in 'blind alley' employment.[37] Yet, crucially, the employment of children outside school times was viewed as 'positively beneficial' provided that it was undertaken within set and clearly defined standards. Provided, in other words, that it was regulated.

The first piece of legislation dealing with 'out-of-school'

employment was the Employment of Children Act 1903. This did not attempt to stop children working, but introduced controls on their out of school labour activities. The legislation also legitimated some work activities and, by introducing controls, identified tasks and conditions that represented 'legal and regulated working' for children. This was exceptionally important in the process of identifying a work arena which was deemed particularly suitable for children and which could be adapted to fit the demands of school attendance. This legislation therefore, was central to 'deproblematising' the issue of child labour, of portraying it as a regulated and healthy pastime and not an exploitative labour activity.

One of the consequences was that child labour disappeared from the social research agenda. Recent historical research, however, suggests that children continued to work in a range of activities through out the economy.[38] Cunningham argues that while the main sectors of child employment were those identified as 'children's jobs', children were still found working in many 'adult' areas of employment. As a consequence of the 1903 act, the control of children at work was constructed around national statute and local byelaws. This was further strengthened by the Employment of Children and Young Persons Act (1933) and its Scottish equivalent from 1937. Cunningham suggests that the regulation of child labour in practice was always rather haphazard and the demands of the local economy were often prioritised over the formal adherence to child labour regulations.[39] In agricultural regions, for example, the seasonal requirement for workers often meant that children were employed at times, in conditions and in jobs from which they were formally prohibited. Further, children could still be found working in a range of factories and mills despite the changing legal environment.[40]

Perhaps one of the most significant changes to have taken place within the child labour market during the twentieth century occurred in the post-second world war period. In the nineteenth and early twentieth centuries, child labour was an overwhelmingly working-class activity. Indeed, as was suggested earlier, it was often among the poorest and most oppressed sections of the working class that child labour exploitation was at its most severe. By the 1950s and 1960s, however, it would seem that a subtle change started to take place in childrens employment. Increasingly children from more affluent working and middle class homes started to take jobs.[41] The developing youth consumer market and culture increasingly required children to have access to money to buy clothes, records and a variety of cultural and consumer goods. In this climate it would seem that some children from more affluent backgrounds started to take jobs.

Of course, some children still worked because of poverty, as indeed some children today work to alleviate their own or their family's poverty. But other children increasingly worked for other reasons. That this was so is perhaps not surprising. After all, work is a central value within present society. Work, it is claimed, teaches children a number of 'valuable lessons', such as responsibility or how to 'handle money'. And child labour is no longer viewed as a serious social problem. As a consequence, children from a range of social backgrounds have entered the labour market, though their motivations for doing so, and the types of work tasks they do, are likely to vary depending on their social class origins.

THE LAW AND CHILD LABOUR TODAY

The employment of children in Britain today is still formally regulated by the Employment of Women, Young Persons and Children Act (1920) and (more significantly) the Employment of Children and Young Persons Act (1933/1937), as amended by various local authority byelaws. The extent to which local authorities have developed child labour byelaws varies enormously. Generally, across the country the legal situation is a confusing muddle. Children cannot work below the age of 13, except if working under direct parental supervision in light agricultural or horticultural tasks when they can work from the age of 10. They cannot work before 7am (though those undertaking the most common jobs of milk and newspaper delivery often do) or after 7pm. On school days and Sundays they cannot work for more than two hours, on Saturdays and school holidays their working day can vary as a result of their age: 13 and 14-year-olds can work no more than five hours, 15-year-olds can work for eight. The confusion the system has bred is well documented.[42] It has also brought Britain's child labour laws into conflict with a number of international and European agreements on working children.

There are three relevant international bodies whose agreements potentially affect child labour law. First the International Labour Office (ILO) which was originally set up in 1919 as a consequence of the Treaty of Versailles has passed a series of recommendations and conventions on a range of work-related issues which member countries (of which Britain is one) are asked to adopt. With regard to child labour, the ILO has put considerable effort into obtaining signatories to its Minimum Age Convention number 138 and its accompanying Recommendation number 146. Passed in 1973, the main aims of the Convention and Recommendation are to:

> pursue national policy to abolish child labour; set minimum age for employment or work not less than the age of completion of compulsory schooling and in any case not less than 15 years; progressively raise minimum age to level consistent with the fullest physical and mental development of young persons; set minimum age for work likely to harm health, safety or morals at not less than 18 years.[43]

To date the British government has failed to sign Convention 138 or Recommendation 146.[44]

A second international treaty, the United Nations Convention on the Rights of the Child (1989), demands that all signatory states make 'the best interests of the child'a primary consideration in all policies that affect children. According to Myers:

> This means that governments need to be able to show that their child labour policies ... do in fact serve the best interests of the country's children ... [T]his is normally understood to mean that such policies effectively protect children's well-being and promote their physical, mental and social development.[45]

Given the evidence on child labour in Britain (see Chapter 1), it is not clear to what extent Britain, a signatory to the Convention, is actually fulfilling its obligations and looking after 'the best interests' of the working child.

Finally a European Community (EC) Directive on working children passed on 24 June 1994 aimed to tighten the conditions and regulation of child employment in member countries. During the discussion period prior to the directive being implemented, the Conservative government of the time suggested this represented unacceptable interference in an area of policy best left to national government. They argued that child employment was an issue over which the 'principle of subsidiarity' should apply.[46] As a consequence, the British government managed to obtain a six year 'opt-out' from the Directive, but this meant that legislation would be required in Britain by the year 2000. On 13 February 1998, Paul Boateng (Parliamentary Under-Secretary of State for Health) gave a commitment that the present government would implement the Directive and bring British law into line with the rest of the European Union.

CONCLUSION

Limited space has not allowed many arguments to be developed, but the historical review of child labour in Britain highlights a number of important issues. The exploitation of child labour increased with the development of complex market systems. This reached its high point during the industrial revolution where children worked long hours in very arduous conditions. State regulation of child labour has often been inadequate, partial and poorly enforced. The trends, from the middle of the nineteenth century, which witnessed the removal of children from the workplace represented a 'victory' for working class children; it protected them from the worst aspects of 'naked' capitalism. Yet the critique of child work by social commentators and politicians was only ever partial. Work and labour are central values of modern British society and labouring was always thought to instil good moral values into working class children. The shift to 'out-of-school' work in the last quarter of the nineteenth century allowed children to combine work with schooling. This was the result of a complex process. It partly reflected economic changes to British society, and partly concern that unregulated labour was affecting an important national asset (children as future workers and parents). Schooling was promoted to educate future workers and better enable Britain to compete with Germany and the US, to control unemployed children in inner city areas and to 'socialise' children to the virtues of British society and Empire. By the early years of the twentieth century child labour was viewed as a decreasing problem and increasingly viewed as a healthy and beneficial pastime. It set in stream a way of thinking about child workers which remains dominant today.

NOTES

1   I Pinchbeck, *Women Workers in the Industrial Revolution*, Virago, 1969.
2   *Ibid*; I Pinchbeck and M Hewitt, *Children in English Society*, Vol 1, Routledge and Kegan Paul, 1969; I Pinchbeck and M Hewitt, *Children in English Society*, Vol 2, Routledge and Kegan Paul, 1974; D Fraser,

The Evolution of the British Welfare State (2nd edn), Macmillan, 1984.

3 E P Thompson, *The Making of the English Working Class*, Penguin, 1968, p384.

4 D Levine, *Family Formation in an Age of Nascent Capitalism*, New York, Academic Press, 1977.

5 *Ibid*.

6 *Ibid*, p13.

7 Pinchbeck, 1969, *op cit*.

8 D Defoe, *A Tour Through the Whole Island of Great Britain*, 1724.

9 H Cunningham, 'The employment and unemployment of children in England, c1680-1851', *Past and Present*, 126, 1990.

10 J L Hammond and B Hammond, *The Town Labourer 1760-1832*, Longmans, 1925, p144.

11 *Ibid*.

12 Compare B Taylor, *Eve and the New Jerusalem*, Virago, 1983 and T Cliff, *Class Struggle and Women's Liberation*, Bookmarks, 1984.

13 Compare J Humphries, 'Protective Legislation, the Capitalist State and Working Class Men: the case of the 1842 Mines Regulation Act', *Feminist Review*, 1981, p8.

14 S Horrell and J Humphries, 'Child Labour and British Industrialisation' in M Lavalette (ed), *A Thing of the Past? Child labour in Britain 1800 – the present*, Liverpool University Press, 1998, forthcoming.

15 Cunningham, 1990, *op cit*.

16 E Frow and R Frow, *The Half-Timer System in Education*, E J Moxton, 1970, p11.

17 *Ibid*.

18 Horrell and Humphries, 1998, *op cit*.

19 H Cunningham, 'Combating Child Labour: the British experience' in H Cuninngham and P P Viazzo (eds), *Child Labour in Historical Perspective 1800-1995*, UNICEF, 1996.

20 *Ibid*.

21 C Nardinelli, *Child Labour and the Industrial Revolution*, Indianapolis University Press, 1990.

22 Horrell and Humphries, 1998, *op cit*.

23 B L Hutchins and A Harrison, *A History of Factory Legislation*, Frank Cass, 1903; Pinchbeck 1969, *op cit*; Fraser, 1984, *op cit*.

24 M Lavalette, *Child Employment in the Capitalist Labour Market*, Avebury, 1994.

25 Hammond and Hammond, *op cit*, p183.

26 M Weiner, *The Child and the State in India*, Oxford University Press, 1991.

27 A Fyfe, *Child Labour*, Polity Press, 1989.

28 Cunningham, 1990, 1996, *op cit*.

29 Lavalette, 1998, *op cit*.

30 S Lasch and J Urry, *The End of Organised Capitalism*, Polity Press, 1987.

31 L Harris, 'The UK economy at the crossroads' in D Massey and J Allen (eds), *Uneven Re-Development: cities and regions in transition*, Hodder and Stoughton, 1988.

32 G Stedman Jones, *Outcast London*, Penguin, 1976.

33 House of Commons Inter-Departmental Committee, *Report on the Employment of School Children*, HMSO, 1902, p265.

34 R D Sherrard, *The Child Slaves of Britain*, Hurst & Blackett, 1905, p189.

35 *Ibid*, p.xviii.

36 Inter-Departmental Committee, *op cit*, p270.

37 A Freeman, *Boy Life and Labour: the manufacture of inefficiency*, King, 1914.

38 S Cunningham in Lavalette, 1998, forthcoming, *op cit*.

39 S Cunningham, 'Child Labour In Britain 1920-1970', PhD Thesis (unpublished), University of Central Lancashire, 1998.

40 *Ibid*.

41 S Cunningham, see notes 38 and 39.

42 See, for example, C Pond and A Searle, *The Hidden Army*, Low Pay Unit, 1991; M Lavalette, J McKechnie and S Hobbs, *The Forgotten Workforce: Scottish children at work*, Scottish Low Pay Unit, 1991; Lavalette, 1994, *op cit*.

43 International Labour Office, *Still So Far To Go: child labour in the world today*, ILO, 1989, p2.

44 R Boyd, 'Child Labour within the Globalizing Economy', *Labour, Capital and Society, 27, 2*, 1994; M Lavalette, 'Thatcher's Working Children: contemporary issues of child labour' in J Pilcher and S Wagg, *Thatcher's Children?*, Falmer Press, 1996.

45 W Myers, 'Preface' in S Hobbs and J McKechnie, *Child Employment in Britain*, Stationery Office, 1997, p.vii.

46 Generally, see M Lavalette, S Hobbs, S Lindsay and J McKechnie, 'Child Employment in Britain: policy, myth and reality', *Youth and Policy*, 47, 1995.

3 Earning your keep? Children's work and contributions to family budgets

Sue Middleton, Jules Shropshire and Nicola Croden

This chapter investigates children's participation in paid part-time work outside the family and the contribution which their earnings make to their own and their families' budgets. While limited information has been available previously about the work and earning patterns of children,[1] there has been no recent attempt to collect evidence which can be used to explore the relationship between children's and families' earnings. The chapter is based on analyses of children's responses to a questionnaire which formed part of the 'Small Fortunes' survey.[2] This survey, funded by the Joseph Rowntree Foundation, is the first ever nationally representative survey of the lifestyles and living standards of British children.[3]

A wealth of information was collected from and about 1,239 individual children from birth to 17 years – an overall response rate of 65 per cent on the issued sample. Data was subsequently weighted to be representative of all children in Britain.[4] All results reported here are based on weighted data for the 230 children aged over 11 years who were asked questions about any jobs which they did outside the home (a response rate of 82 per cent).[5] In other words, we have not included work which children do inside the home for which they receive payment or pocket money since both of these represent, to a greater or lesser extent, a redistribution of family income. Table 3.1 summarises the profile of the sample. The numbers in some cells are small and findings related to these should be treated with some caution.

The children were asked questions about:

- the type of job;
- average hours worked each week;
- weekly earnings.

Information about family income is drawn from interviews with the child's parent. What parents spend on the child and what the child spends on her/himself is taken from a diary of expenditure on the child which was kept for one week.

The first section examines the proportions of children who work in Britain and the types of jobs which they do. Secondly, we describe children's earnings, the hours which they work and their rates of pay. Finally, children's earnings are considered in relation to: family income; children's spending on themselves; and parents' spending on children.

Our analysis focuses on how the experience of being a child worker in Britain varies according to the child's social and economic circumstances. There seems to be a view in Britain that part-time work for older children is a 'good thing'. Work is believed to teach children about the world of employment and mark the beginning of financial autonomy. The unspoken assumption is that children's work is not central to the economy of the family, but instead provides the child with extra pocket money or 'pin money' – similar to perceptions of married women's earnings in earlier years. If this were so we might expect no differences to emerge between children from poorer and richer families. (In this analysis we have used living in a family which is in receipt of income support or in a one parent family as proxies for relative poverty. Lone parent families account for over 10 per cent of the poorest decile of families in the UK[6] and are over-represented among the persistently poor.)

On the other hand, it may be that children from poorer families are more likely to work. They might feel the need to contribute to a restricted family income; to enable parents to spend less on them; or to improve their personal economic circumstances by working to pay for things which their parents cannot afford to buy them. Conversely, children from more affluent circumstances might be more likely to work because they live in areas where more appropriate jobs are available; because their parents have the knowledge, experience and contacts to assist them in gaining part-time employment; or because their parents are more willing for them to work.[7]

In what follows we explore these assumptions and ideas in an attempt to provide a more accurate picture of the role of children's work in their lives and in their families' circumstances.

TABLE 3.1 **Profile of the sample**

	In work	Not in work	Base
All	83	146	229
Girls	42	65	107
Boys	41	81	122
11-12 years	12	54	66
13 years	10	28	38
14 years	21	30	51
15 years	27	22	49
16 years	13	12	25
Lone parent	27	71	98
Two parent	56	75	131
On income support	17	35	52
No income support	66	111	177

CHILDREN WHO WORK AND WHAT THEY DO

WHO WORKS?

Almost two-fifths of children aged over 10 years in our sample do some form of paid work outside the home (Figure 3.1). Although variations in sample sizes and characteristics make comparisons difficult, this is similar to earlier findings.[8] Gender differences are small but girls are slightly more likely than boys to have part-time jobs. As might be expected, older children are more likely to work than younger children. By the age of 15 years over two-thirds of children have at least one part-time job, but the proportion then falls. A similar trend has been noted in earlier research and may be related to the pressure of formal examinations.[9] However, our data show that girls are far more likely than boys not to work by the age of 16 years, perhaps suggesting that girls take the prospect of imminent exams more seriously than boys.

Despite the expected concentration of work among older children, 16 per cent of children aged between 11 and 12 years are regularly involved in part-time jobs. Some of these children are working in potentially hazardous jobs and so are likely to be illegally employed (see below).

FIGURE 3.1: **Who works?**

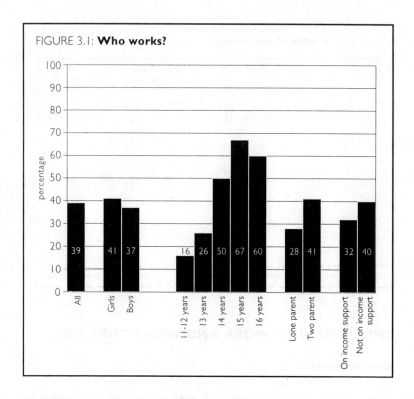

Variations in employment rates are also apparent between only children and those with brothers and/or sisters. Only children (45 per cent) are more likely to work part time than children with either older (36 per cent) or younger (38 per cent) siblings. Possibly parents with only one child are able to give more of their time to assist their child with finding appropriate work than are parents with more than one child.

Children living in two parent families or in families not on income support are more likely to work than those in one parent families or in families on income support (Figure 3.1). Less than one-third of children from families in receipt of income support have part-time jobs, compared with two-fifths of children living in non–income support families. The difference between children living in one and two parent families is more pronounced, with children in two parent families being almost one-and-a-half times more likely to work than those in one parent families.

It seems, therefore, that older children, only children and children in two parent families or families not on income support are most likely to be involved in paid part-time work. To explore further the inter-relationships between working and each of these characteristics we used a logistic regression model (Table 3.2).

TABLE 3.2 **The likelihood of children working**

The reference child is male, 11–12 years old and has no brothers or sisters. He lives in a lone parent family receiving income support

	Odds of working part time
Girls	1.03
13 years	2.11*
14 years	5.48*
15 years	12.53*
16 years	9.65*
First born	0.78*
Later born	1.22*
Two parent family	2.20*
Not on income support	0.91

* = significant, p< 0.05

The model confirms that the likelihood of being employed part time increases with age, with children aged 15 and 16 years being almost 13 and 10 times more likely to work part time than children aged 11–12 years. Children living in two parent families are more than twice as likely to be employed than are children in one parent families, irrespective of other family circumstances. Living in a family on income support has no significant effect on whether or not children work and girls are no more likely to work than boys. Finally, the model indicates that the odds of being involved in part-time work are not necessarily increased for only children. Later born children are 1.2 times more likely to be employed than only children, but first born children are only 78 per cent as likely to work as only children.

We can only speculate why children in two parent families are more likely to have part-time jobs than those in one parent families. As mentioned earlier, it may be that children in one parent families are more likely to live in areas with fewer job opportunities than other children, or they may have to take on more responsibilities at home, for example caring for siblings; or that lone parents are less able to help their children to find work, or that they are less willing for their children to work.

HOW MANY JOBS?

A small but significant minority of children have more than one part-time job. More than one in seven children (14 per cent) who are involved in paid work have two jobs and a further 5 per cent have three jobs. Interestingly, a larger proportion of girls.(24 per cent) than boys (14 per cent) have more than one job. Although, as we have shown, children from one parent families are less likely to work, when they *do* work they are more likely to have more than one job (25 per cent) than children in two parent families (18 per cent). There is no difference between the number of jobs held by children in families on or not on income support.

Although a significant number of children have more than one job, the raw numbers in the sample are relatively small. Therefore, data in the remainder of this chapter refers to all jobs which a child has.

WHAT CHILDREN DO

Children were asked to describe the jobs which they do and their responses were coded into the categories shown in Figure 3.2. Paper rounds and babysitting are by far the most common forms of employment for children over the age of 10 years. There are clear differences in the jobs done by girls and boys in this age group, with boys being more likely than girls to have the more physical or manual jobs. For example, 34 per cent of boys who work have a paper round, compared with only 23 per cent of girls who work. In contrast, girls' predominate in traditionally more female jobs, such as babysitting and restaurant work. Thirty-three per cent of working girls do babysitting compared with only 8 per cent of boys; 9 per cent of girls work in restaurants, but only 2 per cent of boys. A number of children are employed in part-time jobs which were impossible to classify into specific categories – these jobs are recorded in Figure 3.2 as 'other'.

As well as it being illegal for children under the age of 13 to be employed, children between the ages of 13 and 16 are not allowed to work before 7am or after 7pm, or during school hours and there are also

restrictions on work which involves lifting, carrying or moving anything heavy enough to cause injury.[10]

In line with the law, no children under the age of 13 years in our sample were employed in business establishments such as shops,

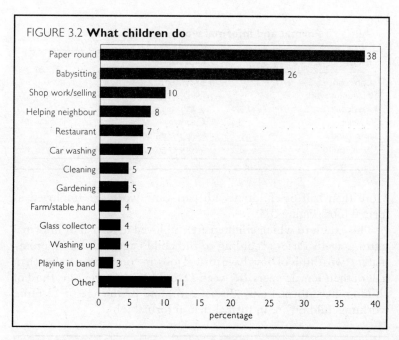

FIGURE 3.2 **What children do**

restaurants and pubs. These younger children tend to be employed by their neighbours, for example, washing cars (10 per cent of 11–12-year-old workers) or generally helping (48 per cent of 11–12-year-olds). However, 5 per cent of 11–12-year-old working children are regularly employed to babysit by people other than their family and over one quarter of working 11–12-year-olds (27 per cent) have newspaper delivery jobs. These jobs can be either physically demanding or performed very early in the morning or late at night. Finally, one in ten children aged 11–12 years are illegally employed as farm/stable hands. It is possible that this is an underestimation of those illegally employed as some children may not have been willing to disclose such information.

FORMAL AND INFORMAL WORK

In order to analyse the effect of differing family circumstances on the work which children do, jobs have been classified into:

• formal jobs, where children work for a business or company;
• informal jobs, such as paid work for neighbours (Table 3.3).

TABLE 3.3 **Formal and informal work**

Formal	Informal
Shop work	Babysitting
Restaurant work	Gardening
Glass collecting	Wash neighbours' car
Washing up	Cleaning
Farm hand	Help neighbours
Paper round	Work in group

More than half of children with part-time work are employed in formal jobs (Figure 3.3).

The extent to which children are employed in formal or informal settings again varies according to the child's age and sex. Approximately two-thirds of boys have formal jobs, in comparison to less than half of their female peers. Between 11 and 12 years, over one-third of children have formal jobs (38 per cent) and by the age of 13 more working children are in formal than informal jobs.

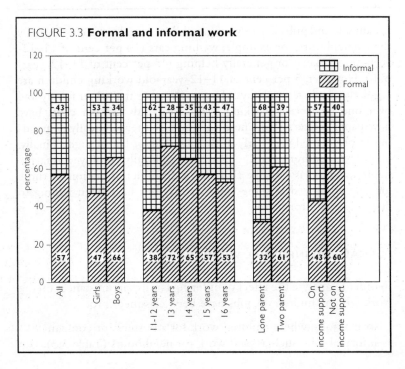

FIGURE 3.3 **Formal and informal work**

Differences also emerge according to whether the child's family is in receipt of income support or not. Working children in families not on income support are much more likely to be involved in formal paid work than are working children in families on income support. Children from two parent families are approximately twice as likely as children in one parent families to be employed in formal jobs. However, further analysis reveals important differences within these groups of children. Children of lone parents claiming income support are almost six times more likely to have formal jobs than are the children of lone parents not on income support. In contrast, children in two parent families on income support are less likely to have formal jobs than children in two parent families not on income support.[11]

CHILDREN'S WORKING HOURS AND WAGES

WORKING HOURS

On average children work for 4.73 hours each week. Approximately one-fifth of children (21 per cent) spend over seven hours a week in paid part-time work which is more likely to be in formal jobs (Figure 3.4). Almost three-fifths (58 per cent) of children working in 'formal' jobs are employed for more than four hours per week compared with just 14 per cent of children working in informal jobs. Children in informal employment are most likely to work for only one or two hours a week (56 per cent).

In general older children work for longer hours than younger children, but one in ten 11–12-year-old children and over one-third of 13-year-olds (37 per cent) work in excess of seven hours a week. There is almost no difference in the hours worked by girls and boys.

The previous section showed that children in one parent families or in families on income support were less likely to have jobs than other children. However, it seems that when these children *do* have jobs they work for longer hours than children in two parent families or families not on income support. Almost one-half of children in one parent families work for more than four hours a week (47 per cent) compared with less than two-fifths of children in two parent families (39 per cent). One-third of children in families claiming income support work for more than seven hours a week compared with only 19 per cent of children in families not on income support.

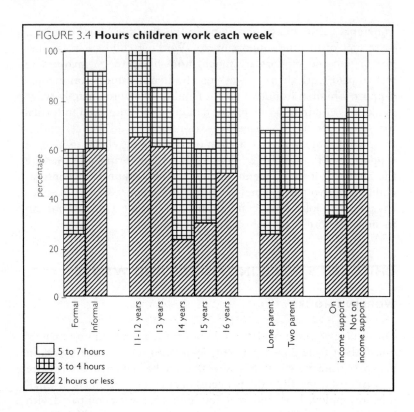

FIGURE 3.4 **Hours children work each week**

5 to 7 hours
3 to 4 hours
2 hours or less

RATES OF PAY

Article 32 of the United Nations Convention on the Rights of the Child states that children and young people have the right to be protected from economic exploitation. The hourly wages shown in Figure 3.5 suggest that working children are not receiving such protection. Overall, children in work are paid an average of £2.22 an hour, but almost one-third are earning £1.25 an hour or less and only 22 per cent are paid more than £2.50 an hour. Although children in formal employment generally fare better in terms of hourly wage rates, one-quarter of children in formal jobs are paid £1.25 or less. At least one in three children are working for less than £1.50 per hour.

Boys receive, on average, better hourly rates than girls (£2.42 and £1.98 respectively) and are more likely than girls to be paid more than £2.50 an hour. Although, as expected, younger children are more likely to receive lower rates of pay than older children, a surprisingly large percentage of 15 and 16-year-olds receive less than £1.26 an hour (21 per cent and 11 per cent respectively).

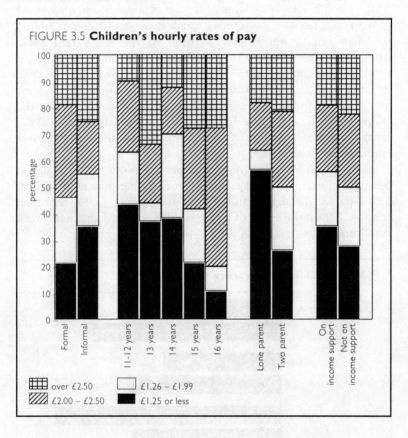

FIGURE 3.5 **Children's hourly rates of pay**

Children in one parent families are particularly disadvantaged in their rates of pay, earning on average 65p less per hour than children in two parent families (£1.65 and £2.30 respectively). Furthermore, children of lone parents are at least twice as likely as children living with two parents to earn £1.25 or less an hour (57 per cent and 26 per cent respectively). Children living in families in receipt of income support are similarly disadvantaged, receiving on average £1.82 an hour compared with the average of £2.27 an hour for children in families not on income support. Children in families on income support are also more likely to receive less than £1.26 an hour (37 per cent) than children in families not on income support (29 per cent).

CHILDREN'S EARNINGS

This section describes children's earnings from work and how hours of work and rates of pay interact to affect these earnings. Children aged between 11 and 16 years earn an average of £9.01 a week. Almost one-quarter of working children (23 per cent) earn £3.00 or less each week and, given the shorter hours and lower rates of pay in informal jobs, it is hardly surprising that these lower earnings are particularly common among children with informal jobs. At the other end of the earnings scale, almost one-quarter of children (23 per cent) earn more than £10 a week, with almost one-third of these children in formal jobs.

Although girls have poorer rates of pay than boys and work almost the same hours, girls' average earnings are higher than boys' (Figure 3.6). Girls are also slightly more likely to earn over £10 a week than are boys. This is the result of a very small number of girls who work very long hours.

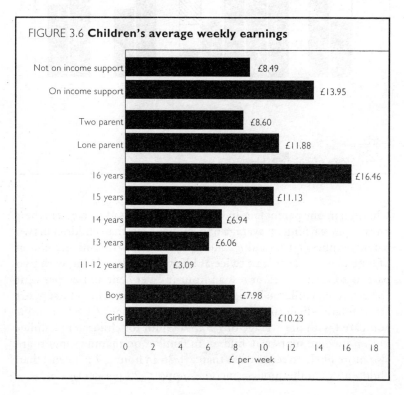

FIGURE 3.6 **Children's average weekly earnings**

Category	£ per week
Not on income support	£8.49
On income support	£13.95
Two parent	£8.60
Lone parent	£11.88
16 years	£16.46
15 years	£11.13
14 years	£6.94
13 years	£6.06
11-12 years	£3.09
Boys	£7.98
Girls	£10.23

We have seen that children in one parent families or families on income support work longer hours for lower rates of pay than other children. The combined effects of these factors on average earnings can be seen in Figure 3.6. Children in one parent families end up with higher average weekly earnings than children in two parent families; children in families on income support earn more than children not on income support. Almost two-fifths of children living in one parent families earn in excess of £10 a week (39 per cent) compared with just over one-fifth of children in two parent families (21 per cent). Children in families on income support are almost two-and-a-half times more likely to be earning over £10 a week than children in families not on income support (48 per cent and 20 per cent respectively).

WORKING FOR PIN MONEY?

In this final section we explore the contribution which children's earnings from part-time work make to the family budget. First, children's earnings as a share of family income are described. This, of course, assumes that children's earnings can be counted as family income (ie, as income which is available to be used for the family's consumption). Our data cannot confirm or refute this assumption since children were not asked directly what they spent their earnings on.

However, we do know how much children spent on themselves during the week in which an expenditure diary was kept. The diary collected information about who paid for items, as well as what was purchased. Again, we do not know whether the money which children spent on themselves came from their earnings or from other sources, such as pocket money provided by parents. But comparing the amounts which working and non-working children spend on themselves will give some indication of the importance of children's earnings to their budgets.

Next we ask whether children's earnings are used to supplement spending by parents or are a replacement for parental spending. Again, our evidence is indirect, relying on a comparison of spending patterns of parents on working and non-working children. If the parents of working children spend the same or more on average than parents of non-working children, then it can be argued that children are simply working to improve their own living standards. Their work is of little importance to their families' budgets. On the other hand, if the parents of working children are spending less on average than the parents of non-working children then it would seem that children are making a real contribution to family budgets.

CHILDREN'S EARNINGS AND FAMILY INCOMES

Overall, the earnings of children who work make up 2 per cent of the total net weekly income of their families. The average earnings of children in one parent families or families on income support are three times larger as a share of family income (6 per cent), than children in two parent families or families not on income support (2 per cent). This is inevitable given that children from one parent families or families on income support earn more on average and have lower average family incomes than other children.

In order to disentangle the effects of variations in children's earnings and family incomes we compared the differences between the incomes of families with working children before and after their earnings are taken into account. Before children's earnings are included, average income in one parent families with a working child are 47 per cent lower than those of two parent families with a working child. Once children's earnings are taken into account this difference decreases to 45 per cent. The same effect is seen for a comparison of the incomes of families on or not on income support – again, children's earnings decrease the difference in average income by 2 per cent.

While these differences are small in percentage terms, the amounts of money which children earn in poorer families could be of great importance to the family budget. Qualitative studies have repeatedly reported that relatively small increases in incomes of around £15 a week would make a major difference to the lives of families on income support.[12] The average of almost £13 a week earned by working children in families on income support could be making a significant difference to their families' living standards. Whether poorer families should have to rely on their children's earnings is, of course, another matter.

CHILDREN'S WORK AND SPENDING

Children's earnings will only improve their families' living standards if they use at least a proportion of their earnings to provide for their own needs, thereby freeing resources which parents would otherwise have to spend on them. If this is so, we might expect working children to spend more on themselves than non-working children, and the parents of working children to spend less on their children than the parents of non-working children.

The larger children's earnings, the more they spend on themselves. This relationship is statistically significant – in other words it is unlikely to have occurred by chance. Figure 3.7 compares the spending patterns of working and non-working children. Overall children who do not work spend only one-quarter as much on themselves as children who work. These differences are clear for children in both one and two parent families, and whether or not the family is on income support. However, working children in families on income support spend 87 per cent more on themselves than non-working children in similar families. Figure 3.7 also shows that working children in one parent families or families on income support spend far more on themselves than working children in two parent families or families not on income support, while the differences for non-working children are very much smaller. It seems therefore that working children, particularly those from poorer families, are contributing to their own budgets rather than saving their earnings. But are their contributions substitutes for, or additions to, parents' spending?

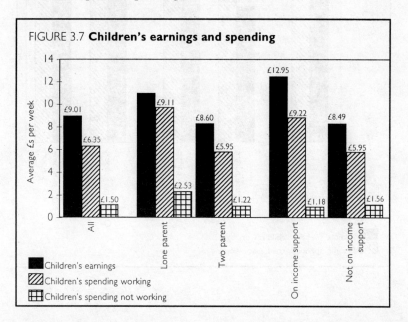

FIGURE 3.7 **Children's earnings and spending**

CHILDREN'S WORK AND PARENTS' SPENDING

Working children receive significantly lower average spending from their parents than non-working children. Overall this difference is 8 per cent, but is greater between working and non-working children in one parent families and in families not in receipt of income support (Figure 3.8). Working children in families not on income support receive slightly more spending from their parents than non-working children in families on income support. The reason for this is unclear but may be connected with the lower levels of spending of all children in families on income support. Hence, parents on income support may be reluctant to reduce what they already feel to be an inadequate level of spending when their child is working.

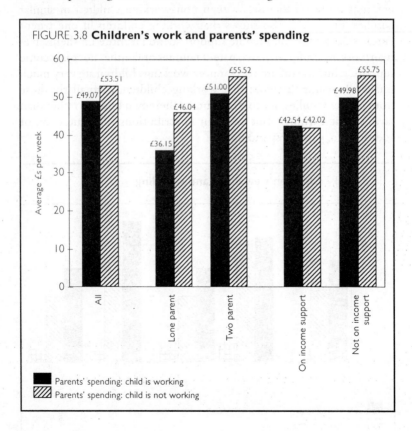

FIGURE 3.8 **Children's work and parents' spending**

All: £49.07 (child is working), £53.51 (child is not working)
Lone parent: £36.15 (child is working), £46.04 (child is not working)
Two parent: £51.00 (child is working), £55.52 (child is not working)
On income support: £42.54 (child is working), £42.02 (child is not working)
Not on income support: £49.98 (child is working), £55.75 (child is not working)

Average £s per week

■ Parents' spending: child is working
▨ Parents' spending: child is not working

CONCLUSION

Almost two-fifths of children in this survey aged between 11 and 16 years have at least one paid part-time job outside the home, rising to over two-thirds of 15-year-olds.

Poorer children are less likely than more affluent children to have paid part-time jobs outside the home. But when poorer children *do* work, despite the lower rates of pay which they receive, they earn on average more than richer children. This is because working children in one parent families or families on income support tend to have either more jobs and/or work for longer hours than other children.

Working children are apparently making a significant contribution to their families' living standards. Overall the earnings of working children contribute 2 per cent of total family income. But working children in one parent families and families on income support contribute three times as much – 6 per cent. Working children in families on income support earn on average almost £13 per week. Their earnings reduce the income gap between their families and families not on income support. On average working children spend more on themselves and their parents spend less on them than non-working children.

It seems that, far from working for 'pin money', many British children – particularly those from poorer families – are indeed 'earning their keep'. We would argue that working long hours, for poor rates of pay, sometimes in dangerous jobs, is inappropriate for young people. However, to prevent them from working could affect severely both their living standards and those of their families. As in less developed countries, attempts to prevent poor children from working which fail to compensate for the negative economic impact on families are doomed to failure.

NOTES

1   C Pond and A Searle, *The Hidden Army: children at work in the 1990s*, Low Pay Unit, 1991.
2   S Middleton, K Ashworth and I Braithwaite, *Small fortunes: spending on children, childhood poverty and parental sacrifice*, Joseph Rowntree Foundation, 1997. A list of other publications is available from the authors.

3 The survey covered England, Wales and Scotland but not Northern Ireland.
4 Fieldwork for the survey took place between February and June 1995. Further details about the sample, weighting and the contents of the survey are available from the authors. The dataset is to be lodged in the ESRC Data Archive at the University of Essex in Spring 1998.
5 Where percentages do not add to 100 this is because of rounding.
6 A Leeming, J Unell and R Walker, *Lone Mothers*, Department of Social Security Research Report No 30, HMSO, 1994.
7 M Lavalette, *Child Employment in the Capitalist Labour Market*, Avebury, 1994.
8 Pond and Searle, *op cit*.
9 J McKecknie, S Lindsay and S Hobbs, *Child Employment in Cumbria: A Report to Cumbria County Council*, University of Paisley, 1993.
10 Children's Rights Development Unit, *UK Agenda for Children*, CRDU, 1994.
11 The numbers of children in two parent families on income support are small so this finding should be treated with caution.
12 See, for example, E Kempson, *Life on a Low Income*, Joseph Rowntree Foundation, 1996.

4 Children's perspectives on work

Save the Children*

Children working in western countries does not have the high profile that 'child labour' has in 'third world' countries. However, in the UK the extent that children work is significant; in fact, it is the norm for children to work (see Chapter 1). There is a wide range of types of employment, the majority being in deliveries, hawking, retail, farming, catering and babysitting. Although there has been considerable research on the extent and type of work done by children,[1] little is, known about what the children think of the work they do, how important it is to them and what role it plays in their lives. This chapter is based on qualitative research conducted by Save the Children in four areas in the UK with children aged 11 to 16. Throughout this chapter the term children and young people is used interchangeably.

METHODOLOGY AND CONTEXT

In total 90 children took part in one-to-one or paired, semi-structured interviews. They were contacted through youth and community projects associated with Save the Children, and via some schools. The emphasis of this qualitative research was to get an understanding of what children think of the work they do. The sample of young people reflects a great variety of situations, including both rural and urban areas. Some of the people live in very low income

* With contributions from Ruth Campbell, Chris Cuninghame, Suzanne Mooney, Carol Nevison, Bridget Pettitt and Paula Rodgers.

areas and some are from minority ethnic groups. The sample was not randomly selected and is not statistically representative of the population as a whole. The four areas in the UK which the young people in this study come from are:

PETERLEE, COUNTY DURHAM

Twenty four of the young people come from an estate in Peterlee, County Durham. This is a new town developed in the 1950s with a population of 31,200 people. It is an area of high unemployment with 14 per cent male unemployment (over a quarter of men have been unemployed for over a year), and high rates of youth unemployment. The estate where the young people were interviewed is characterised by high indices of deprivation such as unemployment, lone parent families, ill health, crime and drug abuse.

LONDON

Nineteen of the young people interviewed come from London. This group was made up from three minority ethnic groups: Irish Traveller, Vietnamese and Bangladeshi. The Irish Traveller community is well established in London, mainly living on official sites. A minority of Traveller children and young people attend mainstream schools. As a community they face discrimination, especially in terms of access to health and other services, and to employment. The Vietnamese community has been established in South West London for over 20 years, originally arriving as refugees from Hong Kong. The Bangladeshi community in North London is among the more recently arrived minority ethnic groups in the UK. Many families are on low incomes, live in poor housing and face high levels of unemployment. Experiences of racism are a major concern for them.

RURAL SCOTLAND

Seventeen of the young people live in two rural areas in Scotland. Some of these live in or near a small town in the North West highlands. The main sources of employment here are tourism, fish processing and manufacture of tourist goods. Seasonal work is very important, linked to accommodation and catering for tourists. The rest of the sample come from an area where the population is dispersed in crofts and villages. The employment here is similarly related to tourism, plus crofting, forestry and fisheries. The nearest small town is about one-and-a-half hours away by car and the young people attend a school which involves a long bus ride.

BELFAST, NORTHERN IRELAND
Thirty of the young people interviewed are from Greater East Belfast. They were drawn from three locations within East Belfast, two of which are largely characterised by high levels of disadvantage, high unemployment and benefit dependency. Youth unemployment is a particular problem within these areas, with as many as 27 per cent of the 16–24-year-olds never having had a full-time job.

AGE AND SEX OF THE SAMPLE

Overall there was an even split within the sample of males (44) and females (46). This did vary according to region. For example, more girls than boys were interviewed in Scotland, and in the London sample, more boys than girls were interviewed, particularly in the Vietnamese and Bangladeshi communities. The majority of the sample were between 14 and 16 years old, and a third were 13 or under. The 16-year-olds were still in school and below the minimum school leaving age, which means they are under the jurisdiction of the Child Employment Act. Eleven of the children were from the Irish Traveller community, four were Bangladeshis and four were Vietnamese.

TABLE 4.1 **Age breakdown of the sample**

Age	male	female	total
11	2	4	6
12	5	1	6
13	6	10	16
14	12	7	19
15	10	15	25
16*	9	9	18
Total	44	46	90

* Under minimum school leaving age

WORK EXPERIENCE OF THE CHILDREN

DEFINITION OF WORK

For the purposes of this research we defined 'work' as being paid work or work that is not paid, but for which an adult would get paid. This fairly narrow definition excludes domestic work, such as helping out around the home, which brings a gender bias to the research since traditionally girls are more likely than boys to be involved in this kind of work. The rationale for using this definition was to ensure the direct policy relevance of this research, as much of the legislation around working children in the UK relates to children in paid employment outside the home.

TABLE 4.2 **Work experience of the children by region**

Region	currently working	had worked in the past	never worked	total
Scotland	8	6	3	17
London	13	4	2	19
Belfast	9	17	4	30
Peterlee	10	10	4	24
Total	40	37	13	90

Just under half of our sample were currently working in some way, and a further 41 per cent have had experience of some type of paid work. Less than a quarter had no experience of work.

TYPES OF EMPLOYMENT

Young people were doing a wide range of jobs. These included: babysitting, delivering newspapers or milk, working in a market, kitchen work, waiting/waitressing, taking orders at a take-away, walking dogs for a kennel, gardening, hairdressing, shop work, house-sitting, building work, carpet laying, selling carpets door to door, teaching dance and aerobics, hotel work, cleaning, selling fish they had caught, working in a nursing home, as a musician, stable hand and swimming pool attendant.

The most frequent jobs were babysitting and delivery work

(which is consistent with findings in other studies – see Chapter 1). Babysitting was done more often by girls than by boys and took place in all areas. However, there were different attitudes towards babysitting. In the Belfast study, only a few children mentioned it as work straight away, whereas a further 15 mentioned it as a hobby which earned them money. In Peterlee, however, it was definitely regarded as a job. Some of the Traveller girls felt that they couldn't ask for money for babysitting.

The range of jobs that the London young people from minority ethnic groups undertook was similar to the other children in the study (babysitting, paper rounds, shop and restaurant work). However, the Travellers were involved in a wider range of work activities.

REASONS FOR WORKING

The main reason for working for almost all the young people interviewed was to earn money. Many young people also talked about enjoying the work they did, speaking of it as a way of killing time and 'keeping them off the streets'. They also felt that they were gaining work experience and were given responsibility.

MONEY

'Well personally I'm very tired of having no money.'
Female, 14, Scotland, not working

'Mainly because I had no money, I just wanted some money...'
Male, 14, Scotland, Kitchen porter

Almost all the children gave money as their primary reason for working. The importance of money is reinforced by children who did not particularly enjoy the work but did it just for the money:

'The paper round ... do you enjoy it?'

'Not really, no ... but the money does come in handy.'
Male, 14, London, newspaper deliverer

Most of the young people described using money to buy things for themselves, like clothes and CDs, and going out and socialising, and spending on leisure. They talked of the opportunities the money gave them. The activities they described were all important areas of young people's lives outside school and work.

Many of the children saved their earnings. This might be for expensive leisure items (such as fishing-rods) or for holidays and presents. Saving for Christmas was particularly important for the Scottish children owing to the seasonal nature of the work (summertime only). One boy talked of saving for a car and for driving lessons when he was 17 (in two years), as transport is a key issue in an isolated area. Several children mentioned saving for the future, some for university. Several Traveller boys talked about saving money ready for getting married and setting up home when they were older.

'What do you do with the money?'

'Put it in the bank ... When I'm 15 I'll get married, pay for my wedding, and buy a van – and some carpets.'
Male, 11, London, carpet seller

CONTRIBUTIONS TO THE HOUSEHOLD INCOME

Although most of the respondents talked about spending money on themselves, for some this was also seen in the context of lack of funds in the home. Many of the young people spent money on essential items such as school books, shoes and clothes.

'...my mum only works part time and my little brother is growing really fast so he needs loads of clothes and everything ... It's just like we all work for our own money really, we just like to have our own money...'
Female, 15, Scotland

'Just for the money, because I like buying clothes and my mum can't give me loads and loads of money ... so I save up to get clothes.'
Female, 14, Scotland

'I'll see what I can buy for school – like pencils, or books and all that.'
Male, 13, London

Some of the children put their money directly into the household pool. One young boy said that he gave some of his wages to his parents for board.

'Sometimes I give money to my parents if they're short, 'cos they are feeding us.'
Female, 16, London, carpet seller

'Hawking (selling carpets) money, I give half to my mother.'
Female, 14, London, carpet seller

'Some of it goes into the bank or maybe I go out at weekends ... and I give mummy some of it ... She's not getting very much money and so I help her.'
Female, 16, Belfast

'Sometimes I give her (mother) money. Sometimes I need the money for school and all.'
Male, 13, London

MONEY AS INDEPENDENCE

For some young people, earning their own money is a matter of gaining independence from their parents:

'Well I want the money, and I'd rather earn money by doing something than just being given it.'
Male, 14, Scotland, garage attendant

'I just did it for the money. I just spend it. Otherwise, I have to ask my mum for the money.'
Male, 14, London, newspaper deliverer

Beyond earning money, however, children and young people gave many other reasons for working. One of the most often quoted was an opportunity to get out and to relieve boredom.

'To get some money at the end of the week. It gets you out, stops you being bored ... getting to know people.'
Male, 14, Belfast, newspaper deliverer

'There's nothing to do round the home, it's so boring. You know where I live, I've got no one my age to talk to.'
Female, 16, London, carpet seller

'It gives me something to do in the holidays because there's not much for young people to do round here.'
Female, 14, Scotland, waitress

'... people here get very bored very easily because there's nothing to do, literally nothing to do.'
Female, 15, Scotland, waitress

'It gives me something to do instead of sitting in the house or playing with the computer ... and I really like doing it.'
Male, 15, Belfast, paper deliverer and builder

'I didn't do it for the money though, I did it because I enjoyed it. It killed some time.'
Male, 12, Peterlee, paper deliverer

Other young people saw their jobs as useful ways of gaining experience of working life, and to help get other jobs later on.

'You get to know how to work in a team, like with the other staff there, and it's something to write down when you're going for another job ... like experience.'
Female, 15, Scotland, campsite receptionist

'It earns me a bit of money and I get the responsibility of being a waitress and how to take orders and so I'll know when I get older how to do it.'
Female, 16, Belfast, waitress

'Just to get used to what I'll be needing to do when I leave school.'
Male, 15, Belfast, waiter

Others describe being treated more like an adult and being given more responsibilities, and being able to show that they were reliable.

'It gives you responsibility when you're babysitting. I used to babysit a two-year-old and you have to be aware of what's going on around you.'
Female, 13, Peterlee, babysitter

'I think that by working it shows you are reliable.'
Female, 16, Peterlee, babysitter

The reasons children gave for working were money, and the opportunities this money provided for them – to relieve boredom, to socialise with their friends and to gain experience and respect. Interestingly, the reasons for working were shared across gender and ethnicity. The Irish Traveller, Bangladeshi and Vietnamese young people all gave similar reasons for working – earning money, socialising and gaining experience.

WHAT DO CHILDREN THINK OF THEIR WORK?

It is clear from much of what the young people said that work plays an important role in their lives. There was little ambiguity in their minds about whether they should work. For example, over half the young people interviewed thought that young people their age should have some sort of job.

ENJOYING THE WORK

As highlighted above in the reasons for working, many young people talked about enjoying the work they did. Getting out and meeting people is a key element of working for these young people – both meeting new people and being able to socialise with their friends as they work.

> *'I love going out and meeting people and being able to talk to them.'*
> Female, 15, Scotland, waitress

> *'You meet people, all people of different nationalities you wouldn't normally meet, so it's quite interesting speaking to them.'*
> Female, 15, Scotland, campsite receptionist

> *'We only get to see each other every few days but we love seeing each other and messing about ... We go off (selling carpets) to have fun as well, but we get money as well like. If we get our money we mess about, but if we don't get money we still mess about.'*
> Female, 14, London, carpet seller

> *'I just like the work. I like talking and getting on with people.'*
> Female, 16, Peterlee, hairdresser

One young person also talked about the job satisfaction she gained from doing the work in a nursing home.

> *'You get a lot of job satisfaction. I really loved working in the home, because they all knew my parents and my grandparents and my great-grandparents ... it's just like you really feel you're doing some good.'*
> Female, 15, Scotland, waitress (who previously worked as a care assistant)

Other benefits gained from working mentioned by children were gaining more respect from parents and getting fitter and stronger doing a paper round. Several babysitters talked about enjoying being with children.

THINGS NOT ENJOYED ABOUT THE WORK

It would be wrong to describe too rosy a picture of children's experiences and perspectives of their work. Not all the children enjoyed the work they did:

> 'Every Saturday you had to do the same job over and over again and I got really bored.'
> Female, 14, Scotland, cleaner

Many of the children doing paper rounds said how tiring the work was – carrying heavy papers, having to get up early and then rush to get the round completed before school. Some young people who did milk or paper rounds talked of lack of sleep.

> 'Like after school you're pretty tired, you have this mass of work, piles of paper waiting for you.'
> Male, 14, London, paper deliverer

> 'You'd have to get up really early – tired – and sometimes you'd forget the number that you'd have to deliver and the owner'd have a go at you. You have to carry them on your bike and the papers are really heavy.'
> Male, 13, London, paper deliverer

Fear of dogs was an issue both the paper deliverers and the door-to-door carpet sellers. Some of the young people described their work as stressful when they were worried about getting things wrong or when work was too hectic.

> 'Sometimes I feel like fainting, feel just like dying there and then because it is really stressful.'
> Female, 16, Belfast, waitress

> 'It is really hard – really tiring – you have to run up and down stairs with trays and clear trays and you've to hoover and you've to do everything and I think that it's really hard.'
> Female, 16, Belfast, waitress

A few of the babysitters talked about the stresses of working. One described how worried she was looking after a new born baby, and that she felt that she had to constantly check that it was all right.

> 'When I was looking after H's baby I was just coming out of the room and the next minute I'd be back in there checking her again.'
> Female, 16, London, babysitter

Others talked about having problems controlling large groups of children and the fear of the damage that they could do to themselves and to the furniture.

Some girls described being harassed by their employers or by customers when they were waiting on tables.

> *'I handed him a hot plate, I said "it's really hot so you'd better watch your hands," and he said, "Oh I could manage that and I could manage you as well." ... I had no idea what to say to him ... they're completely shameless but it's so embarrassing.'*
> Female, 15, Scotland, waitress

HOW CHILDREN ARE TREATED AT WORK

Fundamental to a child's work experience is how they are treated during their work. The interviewees were asked if they felt they were treated fairly at work. Most of the young people felt they were treated well by their employers, and fairly in relation to their peers. No one mentioned any discrimination on the grounds of ethnicity. There was one comment about gender in relation to pay (see below).

> *'Being responsible, like an adult. I get treated like an adult.'*
> Female, 14, Peterlee, babysitter

Although this was a minority experience, some responses were in terms of how they were treated in comparison with adults. Where children felt they weren't treated well they felt they were often given the worst jobs to do, and that they weren't listened to.

> *'Adults get treated better – the jobs are the same but they would get treated better because employers know they are not stupid.'*
> Male, 16, Belfast, kitchen porter

> *'... 'cos you're younger nobody listens to you. Because there was a girl who worked there, she was an older woman in her thirties and she was skiving off work and left us at the front and it was really busy and I says to her about it and I got told off. So they don't listen to the younger ones.'*
> Female, 15, Belfast, kitchen work

> *'The young person always gets the worst job no matter what, no matter where you work ... you just start at the bottom, sweeping up and making cups of tea.'*
> Male, 16, Peterlee, milkman

*'Any little thing that we do we get wrong [ie, in trouble] but the adults don't.
We do more than the adults do on the farm. We work harder.'*
Female, 16, Peterlee, dog walker

Another young person mentioned that being employed casually
meant that employers need not provide training.

*'I think most jobs adults would do, they would expect sort of training and that,
whereas we are just expected to do anything.'*
Female, 14, Scotland, waitress

This was reflected in the young people's definitions of an adult's job
and a child's job. Key themes that emerged were that an adult's job
requires more experience and qualifications. They were seen as
having more responsibility, and a heavier work load and better
prospects. Level of pay was also a key issue. Children's jobs were seen
to be easier, less taxing and involving shorter hours. There was a
strong feeling that children deserved better treatment from adults in
terms of protection. Seventy of the young people agreed that children
should have special protection (88 per cent of those who commented),
and only one disagreed.

'It's (an adult's job) for real, not a game.'
Male, 13, Peterlee, gardener

'Adults get more responsibility, they sometimes get the more fun jobs to do.'
Female, 15, Scotland, waitress

PAYMENT

The majority of the young people seemed to think that they were
paid a reasonable amount for what they did, although this varied
geographically. More young people in Belfast, Scotland and London
than in Peterlee were happier with their level of pay.

'Yeah, it's OK. Because you only do one hour. You get £10 – that's good.'
Male, 15, London, paper round,

All the young people in Belfast who felt they were not being paid
enough were involved in waiting or kitchen work. The young people
selling carpets were paid out of the profits from any rugs they sold. On
bad days they might earn little or no money at all.

Some young people were aware they were being, or could be,

exploited economically. Some felt they got ripped off by adults, and several mentioned the fact that the pay for young people's jobs is not very good. A few said that adults were being paid more for doing the same work.

> *'I think they are pleased, as an adult wouldn't work for that much money.'*
> Female, 16, Peterlee, babysitter and paper deliverer

> *'Adults get paid more money and children get paid less. They don't know how much they're supposed to get for the job they do.'*
> Male, 14, London, paper deliverer

However, others commented that it was fair that they got a different rate from adults as they had different levels of responsibility. There was an expectation that pay rates would increase with age. In Peterlee, a girl said that the boys got paid more for their paper rounds than she did, and that the reason given to her was that the boys' paper rounds were longer (which she did not believe).

Two children who looked after other people's children described not actually getting paid for it in the end, though they had expected payment. The people were either members of their own family or friends of the family, and they felt unable to complain. In some cases they felt able to then refuse to look after the children if approached again, but not always. One paper deliverer said he was given extra work without getting paid for it, by having to put promotional leaflets inside each of the newspapers before they were delivered.

> *'You have to put in 250 leaflets. You don't get much extra money, you get the basic £5 for 250 papers plus £1.50 for property pages insert – then you're given independent leaflets, no matter how many or thick they are.'*
> Male, 14, London, paper deliverer

WHAT THE CHILDREN WOULD CHANGE ABOUT THEIR WORK

The negative aspects of their work referred to above were reflected in what the children said they would change about it. Mostly they talked about increasing the amount of money they earned, decreasing the length of time they worked and not having to work such late hours. More specific examples were not having to deliver so many papers and not having to confront frightening dogs. One mentioned getting a qualification for her work.

HOW THE WORK FITS INTO THEIR LIVES

In order to get a picture of the role of work in these children's lives, we asked what they would have been doing if they weren't working. Very few young people felt they were missing out on anything when they were working. Many of the responses reflect the enjoyment that the children had in the work and that it offered them opportunities to meet and see other people. This was consistent across all the regions. Answers ranged from watching TV, listening to music, 'nothing much', 'being bored' and doing housework. Some did feel that they were missing out on spending time with their friends, whereas others said that the money enabled them to go out more with their friends.

Many of the children demonstrated that they work out a complex timetable of their work, school work and leisure time.

> '... I work and I do homework and I have set nights that I go swimming and then I've got loads of free time to myself ... In the summertime maybe my family have barbecues with friends and that. If I'm working, then sometimes I could miss them, but they're usually still going on when I come back anyway...'
> Female, 15, Scotland, waitress

Children also talked about negotiating time off and altering their hours at work when they wanted to go out with friends. Some of the boys doing paper rounds could control their hours by choosing how many papers to deliver, or only doing weekly papers rather than daily paper rounds.

Many of the Irish Traveller girls talked about doing domestic work at home when they are not hawking, cleaning the trailers, looking after the children and making food.

> 'Clean and clean and clean and clean ... in the morning, evening, afternoon, noon, in the night, midnight, whatever, cleaning all the time, babysitting, cleaning, babysitting, cleaning ... that's it, that's everything because we're good girls.'
> Female, 14, London, carpet seller

ROLE OF PARENTS

The role of parents in their children's work is significant. Many children worked for their parents, or for their parents' friends. The children recognised the role of their parents and there was a strong feeling amongst them that they should ask their parents' permission to work (74 out of 90 young people agreed with this statement, 83 per cent of those who commented). The majority of young people who worked said that their parents were supportive of their work because they became more financially self-sufficient.

> '*My Mum thinks I should do a job because I'm old enough – for newspapers.*'
> Male, 14, London, paper deliverer

> '*They're all for it – they say I have to get out more to earn more money because they are sick of me always asking for money.*'
> Female, 15, Belfast, paper deliverer

> '*They are proud of me for having a job.*'
> Male, 13, Peterlee, paper deliverer

Some reported their parents being pleased that they were getting some experience of working life and being independent, and that they had something to do. Several young people said that their parents like to think of them working rather than worrying about them getting into trouble.

> '*They think it's good 'cos I learn what it's going to be like in the real world when I leave school.*'
> Female, 16, Peterlee, babysitter

> '*My mum just thought it was good me getting out of the house and doing something.*'
> Female, 14, Scotland, cleaner/waitress

Some parents had reservations about the work their children were doing, especially the hours they do and the impact it might have on their school work.

> '*They don't mind as long as it doesn't affect my school work.*'
> Male, 16, Belfast, glass washer in a bar

In fact, many parents seem to monitor young people's hours of work, ensuring homework is not compromised. Some young people would use their parents as a reason for not working late if employers tried to put pressure on them, and occasionally parents would turn up at the workplace to collect the child at the end of the shift to ensure they got home on time.

LINKS WITH SCHOOL AND SCHOOL WORK

The young people were asked if they felt that their school work was affected by their paid work, and what they thought their teachers thought of them working. All the young people interviewed were of compulsory school age. However, many of the Traveller children were not receiving formal education. A minority of the young people felt their work affected their school work. Those who did tended to be the ones working either very early in the morning (doing deliveries) or those working late at night.

> *'I can't concentrate because I'm so tired and I just feel like going to sleep again when I'm in school. It does affect my school work.'*
> Female, 16, Belfast, waitress

> *'Sometimes I did have quite a lot of homework but I just fitted it in. I'd probably just end up lazing about if I didn't go anyway.'*
> Female, 14, Scotland, cleaner/waitress

In a few cases the impact on school work had led to children giving up their jobs. Many others talked about balancing their homework and school work, and appreciated the diversion from their paid work.

The extent to which the young people had let their teacher know about their work varied considerably, especially on a regional basis. For example, in Scotland they generally felt that their work had little to do with their teachers. Either they did not inform them or, because most of their class worked, the teachers did not make an issue of it. This could be explained by the seasonal nature of the work, mostly during school holidays. In Belfast, most young people thought their teachers did not know about them working and many thought they would not have approved if they had.

> *'They crack up when you work ... they say you shouldn't be working 'cos you're too young.'*
> Female, 15, Belfast, chip shop

One teacher had intervened in a pupil's part-time work because she was too tired at school. In Peterlee most young people believed that their teachers approved of them working. One girl was working part time in a hairdresser's which had been set up as part of a work experience scheme. The children were asked to rate certain suggestions about improving the situation for children who worked, one of which was to include children's work as part of a record of achievement at school. This suggestion was rated quite highly, with 48 per cent of those asked giving it 10 out of 10. This would indicate that children are interested in achieving a more integrated approach to their work and school lives.

HEALTH AND SAFETY ISSUES

The young people were asked whether they felt the work they did was dangerous, and whether they had been given any advice or training by their employers on safety procedures. For those with paper rounds, the major concern was the risk of being bitten or chased by dogs, crossing busy roads – especially in the dark, and the potential danger of being threatened by strangers.

> 'In the winter mornings it was pitch black. We were given fluorescent bags so that people could see us, but the shop never knew if you had finished the round safely. You never had to check in.'
> Female, 16, Peterlee, paper deliverer

Another concern of the young paper deliverers was the weight of the bags, and one young person talked of having to go to the doctor because of a pulled muscle in his chest. The female carpet sellers talked about the risk of being attacked and raped, and of the safeguards that they and their bosses and family used to prevent this.

Babysitters seemed to be less concerned in comparison, but a few mentioned being worried about being left on their own, and about the safety of the children in their care.

> 'If any of them chokes, I'd probably not know what to do, I'd probably panic.'
> Female, 13, Peterlee, babysitter

Young people working in catering jobs were aware of the potential dangers. A few related experiences of being burnt by fat, and the dangers of slipping on wet floors and getting cut by sharp knives and glass.

The level to which young people had been given safety instructions from their employers varied. Some were given instructions as a matter of course, others during the work. Interestingly, although the majority of those who worked in kitchens were told about safety, none mentioned learning about food hygiene regulations.

ROOM FOR IMPROVEMENT: REGULATIONS AND ACTION

The children and young people were asked to comment on elements of the existing rules around working children in the UK, such as the prosecution of employers who contravene the regulations. They were also asked to give their views on potential ideas for improvement, such as a minimum wage. They were asked to sort the following statements into agree, don't know and disagree (see Table 4.3 below).

TABLE 4.3 **Young people's views on regulations**

	Agree	Don't know	Disagree	No comment	Total
There should be a minimum wage for young people under the age of 16	64	12	11	3	90
No young person under the age of 16 should work before 7am	58	3	28	1	90
Adults who break child employment rules should be prosecuted	47	12	19	12	90
No young person under the age of 16 should work more than 2 hours a day on a school day	36	10	35	9	90
Children should be allowed to do any work they want to do	31	4	53	2	90
All young people should get a licence to work	23	11	44	12	90
No young person under the age of 16 should work after 7pm	20	5	64	1	90
No young person under the age of 16 should work more than 2 hours on a Sunday	16	8	65	1	90

ATTITUDES TOWARDS REGULATION

It was clear that most children saw a role for regulating the types of work they should do; few agreed that children should be able to do whatever work they wanted. The main reason given for this was protection from dangerous work. There was a majority view that employers who break the rules should be prosecuted. Concern about levels and fairness of payment was reflected in the popularity of the minimum wage idea, although this was complicated for many of the young people to understand, especially in the context of having no other rights as employees.

RESTRICTIONS ON HOURS

Many of the regulations we asked about related to the times of day and week that children are allowed to work. None of the regulations had universal approval. A majority (58 out of 89 who commented) felt that working before 7am was too early and agreed that it should not be allowed. However, a much higher proportion (64 out of 89) felt that children should be allowed to work after 7pm. Different time limits were suggested by many interviewees – some said when it gets dark, allowing for different times in summer and winter. Others differentiated between ages, and between term time and holidays. The restrictions on Sunday hours were disagreed with most strongly. Only 16 agreed with them while 65 disagreed. Children had more mixed opinions around the restriction of two hours per day on a school day, with equal numbers agreeing and disagreeing.

SUGGESTIONS FOR ACTION

A range of ideas were put to the children and young people. These were all based around ways of improving the situation of children who work in the UK (see Table 4.4). By far the most popular suggestion, with over half the young people giving it full marks, was the complaints procedure children could use if they were not happy with their situation at work. Second most popular was having a wage slip from their employer giving details of their hours and wage rate, and third was a range of leaflets explaining employment rights. The popularity of these suggestions reflects how often children feel unfairly treated at work, with no means of recourse or discussion.

TABLE 4.4 **Young people's rating of the suggestions**

Suggestion	low rating 0-3	med rating 4-6	high rating 7-10	number of max score	total children asked	mean score (out of 10)	median score (out of 10)
An official complaints procedure for young people of your age if they are not happy with their working conditions	3	8	69	44	80	8.7	10
Wage slips for young people from their employers, giving details of the pay rates per hour	7	9	63	35	79	8.1	9
A range of leaflets explaining employment rights for young people your age	1	13	65	23	79	8	9
A system where young people's work is included in a record of achievement at school	6	0	61	36	77	7.9	9
A club or network for young people of your age who work	5	21	54	10	80	7	8
A licence system so that all people who employ young people of your age have to register	17	18	45	22	80	6	8

CONCLUSIONS

The young people whose views are expressed above come from different backgrounds within the UK. Yet there were great similarities in terms of their attitudes towards work, their reasons for working and the variety of jobs they do. These similarities were striking across both gender and ethnicity. Work plays a key part in their lives. The money is a way of gaining independence, enabling them to participate socially with their friends, buy clothes, eat out and buy leisure equipment. Many of these young people come from low income areas, and some children were contributing both directly and indirectly to their household income. That is, they were either handing over some of their earnings to their parents, or they were buying essential items for themselves or for their school work. Many young people were saving their earnings. For the majority the work represented more than just having the money. It was a way of meeting new people, being with their friends and getting away from home. In some cases it was a key to alleviating boredom. For others it was a way of gaining experience and confidence.

There were also disadvantages to working. Much of the work is tiring and stressful. In some cases young people felt they were not treated fairly, especially compared to the way adults are treated. A few felt they were not given a fair amount of money for extra work. In one case this was related to gender. Some were exposed to dangerous or unpleasant situations. Parents play an important role in monitoring the young people's work, both in terms of sanctioning the work they do, and in protecting them from working long hours.

Most of those interviewed felt that young people should be protected from dangerous work, but that the current regulations are not sensible. In particular the restrictions to working in the evenings and on Sundays were felt to be unreasonable. Suggestions for improvements included being given wage slips from their employers with details of their hours and rates of pay, and having more information about their employment rights. Their main priority was an official complaints procedure.

NOTE

1   S Hobbs and J McKechnie, *Child Employment in Britain: A social and psychological analysis*, Stationery Office, 1997; F Jolliffe, S Patel, Y Sparks and K Reardon, *Child Employment in Greenwich*, London Borough of Greenwich, 1995.

5 Children's contribution to household income: a case study from Northern Ireland

Madeleine Leonard

Over recent years, studies into the participation of school students in the labour market have revealed that working while at school is a typical rather than an unusual experience for many school children in Britain.[1] These studies document that between 20 and 50 per cent of school students under the age of 16 are likely to be in some form of paid employment. Moreover, rather than term-time employment being limited to a few characteristic occupations such as newspaper rounds, the studies reveal that children work in a diverse range of occupations, experience differing work conditions, are paid varying wage levels and work miscellaneous hours.

Such research has yet to be extended to Northern Ireland, where the participation of school students in term-time employment remains a much neglected issue. During 1997, Save the Children in Belfast commissioned John Pinkerton from the Centre for Childcare Research to undertake an exploratory review of existing empirical research on children and work in Northern Ireland. At the end of a thorough research of the likely sources, Pinkerton concluded 'we were still in a state of ignorance'.[2] This 'ignorance' is not surprising. The saliency of the 'troubles' in Northern Ireland continues to preclude academic interest from 'normal' features of inhabitants' daily lives.

By drawing on research in Britain which indicates that two out of every five children are likely to be in employment, Pinkerton surmises that currently around 60,000 children are likely to be engaged in work in Northern Ireland. He concludes that this 'guesstimate' should 'underscore the importance of ensuring that primary research is commissioned on children and work in Northern Ireland as a matter of urgency'.[3]

It is against this backdrop that the study reported on here should be considered. During 1990, I interviewed 122 school students from a low income Catholic estate in West Belfast to determine the extent and significance of term-time employment among school-age children in the area. This small-scale study provides a useful starting point for examining the participation of pupils from economically disadvantaged backgrounds in paid employment. Such a specific focus has been largely absent from many of the British studies which concentrate mainly on pupils from diverse geographical areas (even within specific towns and cities). However, the disadvantage of this exclusive focus is that the research cannot be considered as representative of the typical work experiences of young people from low income households in Northern Ireland. Much wider research into the experience of school students from different localities is urgently needed, and Save the Children has begun the process of collecting such information. Nonetheless, the case study presented here provides a useful analysis of the importance of paid employment in the lives of pupils from similar economic backgrounds who live in close proximity to each other, and the findings can be utilised for future comparative purposes.

The chapter begins by providing a brief description of the estate where the research took place. This will be followed by a brief outline of the characteristics of the pupils who took part in the study. The following three sections will document the types of work the pupils engaged in, their hourly wage rates and the degree to which their earnings contribute to their household incomes.

BACKGROUND TO THE STUDY

I chose the estate where the research took place because it represented one of the peak unemployment regions in Northern Ireland. A range of studies consistently indicated higher than average rates of adult male unemployment on the estate.[4] These studies make depressing reading, portraying an estate characterised by economic insecurity and poverty. Boal *et al*'s research, for example, involved a comparison of 97 areas of special need in Northern Ireland. The estate where my research took place came top of their list on a range of negative indicators, including unemployment, poverty levels, overcrowding, mental disability and higher than average sickness rates among children and adults. In 1990, I undertook a survey of one in four (150) households in the area. Husbands and wives were interviewed in each household where appropriate, as was the primary adult in lone parent households.

The main purpose of the interviews was to ascertain the levels of unemployment among adult males and females from the estate and then to assess their ability to manage on welfare benefits. This latter focus involved looking at the range of work opportunities for adults in the informal economy, the extent of 'self-provisioning' within households (eg, doing their own decorating and repairs) and participation in reciprocal transactions within the estate (eg, washing and ironing a neighbour's clothes in return for decorating), and in voluntary work. In all, 118 men and 124 women living in 150 households were interviewed.[5] Of the 118 men in the sample, only 28 (24 per cent) had access to formal employment. The rest qualified for a varying range of welfare benefits. Of the 124 women interviewed, only 24 (19 per cent) had access to formal employment. Managing on welfare benefits was therefore a typical feature of life for the majority of households.

The research was also concerned with the participation of school students in paid employment. The principals of the three schools servicing the area allowed me to interview pupils individually about various aspects of their lives on the estate and where appropriate their employment experiences.

While one of the primary aims of the research was to ascertain the extent and significance of paid employment in the lives of school-age children from the estate, it must be emphasised that this was by no means the only issue the research was concerned with. The main purpose was to examine the importance of several forms of work in the lives of individuals from an area characterised by widespread unemployment. This involved asking adults and pupils about their involvement in a wide range of economic activities rather than simply restricting the analysis to paid employment. The pupils were also asked about their attitudes to living in Northern Ireland, their particular experiences of living on the estate (a republican stronghold), their participation in voluntary work, household work, reciprocal transactions and their future plans in terms of marriage and career. Given this wide remit, the sections relating to participation in paid employment had to be partial, concentrating mainly on types of jobs undertaken, hourly wage rates, working conditions, and the uses to which earned income was put. The remainder of the chapter will draw on this material.

BACKGROUND CHARACTERISTICS

One hundred and twenty-two pupils between the ages of 14 and 17 were interviewed. I chose to concentrate on this age range for two reasons. First, my intention was to aim for a total sample of school students within specific age groups from the estate. Preliminary meetings with school principals indicated that if this age range was set too wide, permission to interview all pupils who fell within the appropriate categories would be denied. This was mainly because I wanted to interview each pupil individually and each interview was to last between 30 minutes and one hour. My second reason for focusing on this age group was because I felt that term-time employment might be more significant for older school students. This judgement was influenced by the fact that many businesses refuse to employ workers without a national insurance number, and you have to be 16 years of age to qualify for one. Other research indicated that term-time employment was an important feature of older pupils' lives. For example, Hutson, from a study of nine firms in Swansea, found that one-third of the total workforce in supermarkets and stores and two-thirds of the total workforce in fast food chains were sixth formers.[6] Because of these factors, I decided to split the sample into four main groups – boys and girls aged under 16 and boys and girls over 16. Table 5.1 represents an age breakdown of the pupils interviewed.

TABLE 5.1 **Age range of school pupils**

	Under 16	Over 16
Male	35	30
Female	34	23
Total	69	53

Just over one quarter of the boys' fathers were in full-time employment, while slightly under one fifth of the girls' fathers were employed full time. Most of the school pupils lived in households where unemployment was the norm – 63 per cent of the boys' fathers and

62 per cent of the girls' fathers had been out of work for more than five years. Hence, most pupils lived in households dependent on welfare benefits.

TYPES OF PAID EMPLOYMENT

Thirty males (44 per cent of the sample) and 21 females (40 per cent) had some form of part-time employment. In other words, one in three pupils worked in paid employment outside of school hours. These participation rates are comparable to studies carried out in Britain. When the sample is divided into those under 16 and those over 16, the division reveals that 53 per cent of the males and 38 per cent of the females who engaged in part-time employment were under 16 years of age. The following table gives a breakdown of the types of jobs held by pupils from the estate.

TABLE 5.2 **Types of jobs undertaken**

Job	No of males	No of females
Construction work	6	0
Clerical work	0	1
Newspaper deliveries	5	0
Coal and milk deliveries	8	0
Working in shops/supermarkets	3	9
Selling from market stall	3	0
Door-to-door selling	2	0
Working in a pub	3	2
Working in café/restaurant	0	6
Hairdressing	0	3
Total	30	21

It is clear from the above table that gender influences the type of work undertaken. More than half the boys interviewed were employed in just two types of occupation: construction work and coal, milk or newspaper deliveries. Only three boys compared to nine girls worked in shops or supermarkets. Moreover, the interviews revealed that the boys who worked in supermarkets were involved in stacking shelves and collecting trolleys, whereas the girls were more likely to be serving customers. Other jobs, such as hairdressing and working in cafés and restaurants, were the sole preserve of girls.

Thus, the first labour market experiences of school students from this study were gender specific, which may have an impact on their later employment.

HOURS WORKED AND WAGE LEVELS

Fourteen of the boys and nine of the girls worked under 10 hours a week, while the remainder of the sample worked more than 10 hours. Three pupils worked more than 20 hours a week and stated that they frequently fell asleep during school lessons as a result of either working late at night or in the early morning before school. The majority, however, did not feel that their education was affected by their term-time employment. This reflects the general conclusions of the research carried out in Britain. Indeed, McKechnie *et al* found that children who work up to five hours per week seem to perform better than children with no paid work.[7] On the other hand, children who work more than 10 hours per week seem to perform less well than children who do not work. Since I am unaware of the pupils' subsequent examination results, I am unable to ascertain whether working had a detrimental impact. Their perceptions indicate that the majority do not believe this to be the case. However, a report from the Institute of Fiscal Studies for Northern Ireland found that the exam performance of 16-year-olds who worked part time while at school for more than six hours per week was worse than those who did not work.[8]

One of the most disturbing aspects of the data concerned hourly wage levels. Table 5.3 presents a breakdown of the wage rates for pupils from the estate.

TABLE 5.3 **Pupils' hourly wage rates**

Amount	No of males	No of females
Under 50p	4	3
50p	6	2
£1	7	10
£1.50	8	3
£2	5	2
£3	0	1
Total	30	21

Table 5.3 reveals that 10 of the boys and five of the girls earned 50p or under per hour in 1990. This means that even when they worked a substantial number of hours it generated very little income. Only one female and none of the males earned over £3 per hour. Hence, teenage employment was characterised by extremely low rates of pay.

PUPILS' EXPENDITURE AND CONTRIBUTION TO HOUSEHOLD INCOME

The majority of school students I interviewed said they did not contribute directly to household income. This was partly due to the insignificant number of hours worked each week and the low rates of pay. Nonetheless, five pupils stated that their families depended on the income they earned from out-of-school employment. Three of these belonged to one parent households. While the majority of those interviewed lived in households dependent on welfare benefits, research suggests that children of lone parents are more likely to live in poverty, mainly because their welfare benefit entitlements more often fail to meet the household's daily needs.[9] One 15-year-old boy, the eldest of four children, stated that his mother depended on his earnings in order to fulfil the family's basic needs. In this case, the boy gave his total earnings to his mother and in return received what he termed 'extra pocket money'. In the remaining four cases, the pupils themselves decided the percentage of their earnings which would be handed in to the household and the percentage they would retain. Two kept the greater proportion of their wages for their own needs, while the other two gave a higher proportion to their parents. As one boy told me, 'my ma needs it more than I do'.

Focusing on the extent to which pupils contribute directly to the income of their households draws attention away from the ways in which they might contribute indirectly by subsidising or paying for their clothing and leisure activities. This can be illustrated by comparing the purchasing behaviour of pupils with and without jobs. All 122 pupils who took part in the study were asked if they received weekly pocket money from their parents. Forty nine boys and 38 girls said they did, although the amounts given were small, ranging from £1 to £4 per week. Seventeen of the boys and 14 of the girls with part-time jobs continued to receive pocket money.

All the pupils were asked what they typically spent their pocket money on. The majority spent their money on items for immediate consumption such as cigarettes and sweets. Three-quarters of the girls in the sample, as well as purchasing these items, used part of their pocket money to buy make-up and other toiletries. However, when the pupils who had part-time jobs were asked what they spent their earnings on, the majority utilised their earnings to fund their clothing and leisure needs. This took two main forms. First, some pupils took responsibility for buying items that their parents had previously provided for them, particularly clothing. Secondly, pupils purchased non-essential goods and services that their parents would have been unlikely or unable to provide, such as music tapes and trips to the cinema.

Of course, given the low wage rates outlined earlier, the pupils capacity to fund their clothing and leisure needs was severely limited. However, it absolved some parents from the strain of providing additional, 'unnecessary' items. Pupils who worked stated that they could buy items their friends on the estate with no jobs had to do without. In relation to clothing, parents purchased necessary items such as school uniforms, shoes and a limited range of additional clothing. Often, these items were regarded as unfashionable by the pupils and those with wages could spend their earnings on satisfying personal preferences. Of course, this does not mean that working pupils went around the estate wearing Nike trainers and designer sweatshirts. The meagre wages earned by the majority did not stretch to cover the cost of such items. However, the income did allow for the limited purchase of non-essential items.

PUPILS' ATTITUDES TO THEIR EMPLOYMENT

Since most young people work to earn spending money rather than to fulfil basic needs, the low wages they earn are generally not a major source of discontentment. The majority of pupils I interviewed seemed unperturbed by what seemed to me to be highly exploitative wage rates. In some of the worst cases, where pupils earned 50p or under per hour, often they were employed by members of their extended family. Pupils employed through these kinship and social networks seemed grateful that they were being paid for what a number defined as 'helping out'.

Their subsequent descriptions of the nature of their employment seemed far removed from merely helping out. One 15-year-old pupil helped his uncle deliver coal. This involved lifting heavy sacks of coal and slack. He worked on average 20 hours per week and was paid £10 weekly. Another helped his uncle deliver milk. He started work each morning at 6am and worked until 8am, seven days a week, and then helped his uncle to collect payment on Friday evenings. His uncle paid him £15 per week. Of course, there is the possibility that such jobs were deliberately created to assist relatives in financial difficulties, which may have been more acceptable than direct hand-outs. Alternatively, adults may have felt that the bonds of kinship justified the low wage rates paid to minors to whom they were related.

A similar situation arose in relation to children who helped parents with family businesses. In four cases, households on the estate had been transformed into house shops opening from early morning until late in the evening. In each household, children played a fundamental role in staffing the shop, either before attending school in the morning or in the late afternoon or evening when they came home. Where parents are also employers, the status of a child as an employee is difficult to sustain as the child forms part of the family pool of labour. In another three households, women worked informally as dressmakers. Their ability to do this was linked to the involvement of their children in the running of the household. In each case, young women undertook considerable responsibility for housework and the care of other family members. This latter case illustrates the problem of solely concentrating on paid employment outside the household when looking at the issue of children and work. Children may be involved in an extensive range of invisible, internal household activities which are time consuming and dilute their opportunities for paid employment outside the household. While in a number of these cases children do not directly contribute to the upkeep of their households, it is clear that their 'free' labour may play a significant part in achieving some economic security.

A minority of those interviewed did express dissatisfaction with their hourly wage levels but stated that, since a large pool of potential teenage employees is readily available, they had to accept the going rate. Pupils typically are ignorant of their legal rights and their employers' legal responsibilities towards them. Hence, child labour laws are often breached. None of the pupils I interviewed were aware of any legislation governing their employment. A number of the sample were employed off-the-books so, even if appropriate, effective legislation were to be introduced, it is difficult to see how such workers would benefit.

Working informally was a common characteristic among unemployed adults living in the estate. The absence of formal employment opportunities, together with the inadequacy of welfare benefits, motivated many adults (37 men and 24 women) to seek work in the informal economy in order to gain extra income. Their employment conditions mirrored those outlined above for school students. At the time of the interviews (1990–91), the average male wage rate was £2 per hour, while for women it was £1. Adding these paltry sums to welfare benefit entitlements enabled a number of households to fulfil their basic needs rather than live in the supposed lap of luxury sensationalised in media accounts of 'welfare scroungers'.

Examining the work patterns of households rather than individuals adds further complexities to the issue of child employment. It is clear from examining the wage rates of adults who work informally that the seemingly low wages of teenagers is open to question. Some of the formally employed teenagers making £2 per hour earned twice the amount earned by married women working informally as contract cleaners in the city centre of Belfast.[10]

TERM TIME EMPLOYMENT AND FUTURE CAREERS

During the interviews, I asked all the pupils about their future career intentions. This was partly to assess the extent to which term-time employment might pave the way for future full-time employment once they had left school. At the time of the interviews, only one respondent had been offered a permanent job arising from her term-time employment. She worked in an office after school and on Saturdays and told me that, while she would not like to work in an office for the rest of her life, the job offer could lead to better things and would give her a head start in the labour market. One of the boys who worked in a supermarket hoped his position would be made permanent when he left school but, at the time of the interviews, had no confirmation of this. The remainder of the sample either did not want a permanent job or did not think it was likely they would be offered a full-time position.

Since school students tend to see their present work situation as a temporary rather than a permanent feature of their future working lives, they are often more willing to engage in dull, repetitive, menial work without complaint. Drawing on their research findings in the United States, this leads Greenberger and Steinberg to question the usefulness of out-of-school employment for providing teenagers with a means of learning skills, acquiring knowledge or developing values that may have significant future payoffs.[11] However, some pupils may test out future employment plans through out-of-school employment and their experiences may have unintended positive consequences. Ten of those I interviewed adjusted their occupational horizons upwards as a result of being involved in part-time, paid employment. All of this group had intended to leave school at 16 and seek any type of unskilled, full-time employment. However, their aspirations changed as a result of involvement in dead-end student jobs. The following quotes illustrate the teenagers perceptions of their out-of-school employment:

> *All I do all day long is stack shelves – imagine spending the rest of your life doing that.*

> *Well, my job's okay. It gives me a few bob, but if I thought I had to do the same thing for the rest of my life, I'd go nuts.*

> *At the beginning it wasn't too bad, but as each day passes, it becomes more and more boring. It's starting to get on my nerves.*

> *They've got the punishment all wrong here [at school]. If they really wanted the kids to work, they should send them out all over the summer to do the donkey work I had to do. You'd work your arse off then to make sure you don't end up doing that.*

Having access to part-time, paid employment may play a key role in encouraging the above pupils to stay on at school after the minimum leaving age. If pupils can provide for some of their own needs through earning their own income, this may also enable low income households to 'afford' to back their child's decision to remain in education.

CONCLUSION

Assessing the extent to which child employment may contribute to household income is no easy task. Simply concentrating on direct contributions averts attention away from the myriad of ways in which pupils may contribute indirectly to the economic security of their households. In the sample of low income households outlined above, the ability of children to provide for some of their own needs enabled household resources to be directed to more immediate needs. Moreover, through their voluntary labour, some children contributed to the economic viability of small-scale, family-run enterprises and in this way made a fundamental, though invisible, contribution to household income.

While the wage rates of the pupils who took part in this study on first impressions seem highly exploitative, when placed against the economic circumstances of adults on the estate, they appear much less so. This indicates the importance of regional and locality variations in relation to child employment. Well meaning national policies aimed, for example, at introducing minimum wage levels for school-age workers may be inappropriate and damaging to the interests of children from particular areas. Policy attempts to regulate and monitor child employment often ignore the possibility that much child employment may take place in the informal rather than the formal economy and hence escape regulation.

Yet, this does not mean that we should sit back and do nothing. It is clear that children themselves should play a key role in efforts to enhance their employment conditions. This means listening to children from different backgrounds and localities and attempting to incorporate their views and suggestions into recommendations for future action. It is only by examining the diverse experiences of working children and their household circumstances that we can begin to understand the complexities of the issues involved and the lack of alternatives some children face. For the most part of the twentieth century, children's views have been silenced and their contribution to the economy rendered invisible. The fallacy of this position is being increasingly challenged, but it remains the case that much more, particularly qualitative, research into the issue of child employment is urgently needed.

NOTES

1 E MacLennan, J Fitz and J Sullivan, *Working Children*, Low Pay Unit, 1985; C Pond and A Searle, *The Hidden Army: children at work in the 1990s*, Low Pay Unit, 1991; M Lavalette, *Child employment in the capitalist labour market*, Avebury, 1994; M Lavalette, 'Thatcher's working

children: contemporary issues of child labour' in J Pilcher and S Wagg (eds), *Thatcher's Children? Politics, childhood and society in the 1980s and 1990s*, Falmer Press, 1996; M Lavalette, S Hobbs, S Lindsay. and J McKechnie, 'Child employment in Britain: policy, myth and reality', *Youth and Policy*, No 47, 1995, pp1–15; J McKechnie, S Lindsay and S Hobbs, 'Child employment: a neglected topic?', *The Psychologist*, May 1996, pp219-222.

2 J Pinkerton, 'Children and work as an issue in Northern Ireland – setting an agenda', *No Time To Play: local and global perspectives on child employment*, One World Centre for Northern Ireland, 1997, p85

3 *Ibid*, p91.

4 F W Boal, P Doherty and D G Pringle, *The Spatial Distribution of Some Social Problems in the Belfast Urban Area*, Research Paper, Belfast, NICRC, 1974; F W Boal, P Doherty and D G Pringle, *Social Problems in the Belfast Urban Area*, Occasional Paper No 12, Dept of Geography, Queen Mary College, London, 1978; P Doherty, *A Geography of Unemployment in the Belfast Urban Area*, Unpublished PhD Thesis, Queen's University, Belfast, 1977; P McAuley, *Glenside: a study of a community*, Unpublished PhD Thesis, Queen's University, Belfast, 1986.

5 M Leonard, *Informal Economic Activity in Belfast*, Avebury, 1994.

6 S Hutson, *Saturday Jobs: sixth formers earning and spending*, Paper presented to the British Sociological Association Annual Conference, Surrey, 1990.

7 J McKechnie, S Hobbs and S Lindsay, *Educational Impact of Part-time Employment on School Pupils*, Paper presented to the British Psychological Society, University of Strathclyde, Glasgow, 1995, published in *Proceedings of the British Psychological Society*, 4, 2, 1996.

8 *The Belfast Newsletter*, 12 March 1996.

9 J Millar, *Poverty and the Lone-Parent Family*, Avebury, 1989; N Oldfield and Autumn C S Yu, *The Costs of a Child: Living Standards for the 1990s*, CPAG Ltd, 1993.

10 M Leonard, 'The modern Cinderellas: women and the contract cleaning industry in Belfast' in S Arber and N Gilbert (eds), *Women and Working Lives: divisions and change*, Macmillan, 1993.

11 E Greenberger and L Steinberg, *When Teenagers Work: the psychological and social costs of adolescent employment*, New York, Basic Books, 1986.

6

Children at work: healthy or harmful?

Ellen Heptinstall

In European and UK legislation, people under the age of 16 are defined as 'children'. However, while talking to people of secondary school age in my role as researcher, I found that referring to them as children created a barrier between them and adults. I will therefore use the term 'young people' or 'young worker' except when quoting legislation or other sources.

The debate about whether part-time work is good or bad for young people started in the United States and has been dominated by research carried out by a few researchers. Although during the past decade there have been several reports on child employment in Britain, they concentrated largely on the extent of child employment and working conditions. The 'cost and benefits' argument surrounding young workers has only recently been taken up by researchers in the UK.[1]

One factor which largely has been ignored in the debate on whether or not employment is good for young people has been the issue of accidents at work. Although there may be disagreement over the costs and benefits of work to young people, there is no doubt that accidents, no matter how minor, can only be regarded as harmful or potentially harmful. I will therefore reverse the title of this chapter and start by discussing the 'harmful' aspect of work and look at the extent to which young workers may be at risk of injury and other physical harm. The argument will then be broadened out by examining the existing literature on the psychological and educational effects of work on young people.

ACCIDENTS TO YOUNG WORKERS

In the UK, the only official source of information on accidents and injuries to employees under the age of 16 is produced by the Health and Safety Executive (HSE) under the Reporting of Injuries, Disease and Dangerous Occurrences Regulations 1985 (RIDDOR). These regulations require HSE field operations division inspectorates and local authorities to report injuries to employees. The regulations cover the agricultural, manufacturing, construction, public utilities and services sectors. The field operations inspectorates and local authorities depend on reports of injuries from employers and employees.

Figures of injuries are divided into fatal, major and 'over three days'. Major injuries refer to fractures, amputations, serious injury to an eye or loss of sight and any other injury resulting in immediate admission to hospital for more than 24 hours. An 'over three day' injury is defined as an injury causing incapacity for normal work for more than three days. The category 'over three day injury' is likely to overlap to a considerable extent with the 'major injury' category in that many major injuries lead to more than three days off work. It is likely that some relatively minor injuries which would not fall in the 'major injury' category also result in an incapacity for normal work for more than three days.

Young workers aged 16 or under are divided into three categories: employees, youth training (YT) trainees and other trainees. The last two categories are likely to include 16-year-olds who have left school or who are work experience trainees. Figures covering the years 1993 to 1995 are shown in Table 6.1.

TABLE 6.1 **Injuries to employees under 16 years old**
Year 1993/94 and 1994/95(a)
As reported to HSE's field operations division inspectorates and local authorities

Status	1993/94			1994/95 (p)		
	Fatal	Major	Over 3 days	Fatal	Major	Over 3 days
Employees	1	5	4	1	8	10
YT trainees	0	0	4	0	0	3
Other trainees	0	11	9	0	9	9
Total	1	16	17	1	17	22

(a) – years commencing 1 April
(p) – provisional
Source: reports under RIDDOR made to the Health and Safety Executive

The official statistics suggest that the number of severe injuries to employees under the age of 16 is very small indeed. However, there is evidence that the official statistics substantially underestimate the number of injuries. The HSE accepts that there is a problem of under-reporting, in particular of non-fatal injuries. In order to estimate the level of under-reporting by employers, the HSE commissioned questions in the 1990 Labour Force Survey (LFS) and again in the 1993/94 and 1994/95 surveys. Although these surveys did not cover employees under the age of 16, the published figures (see Table 6.2) give an overall picture of the level of under-reporting by employers.

TABLE 6.2 **Percentage of all non-fatal injuries not reported to HSE and local authorities**

Industry	1990 (%)	1993-95 (%)
Agriculture	79	69
Energy and water supply	21	37
Manufacturing	58	48
Construction	60	60
Distribution, hotel and catering	82	73
Transport and communications	62	39
Business	92	89
Public administration/defence	27	33
Education	70	55
Health	75	63
Personal/consumer services	85	79

Source: Health and Safety Executive

The results show that under-reporting of non-fatal injuries is common in all industries, but there are large differences between industries. Many young people work in distribution services delivering newspapers and milk, and in shops and businesses. Both distribution and business services were among the areas with the highest rates of non-reported injuries. On the basis of the information provided in Table 6.2, the actual number of reportable injuries to workers under the age of 16 could be expected to be at least three times higher than the number of reported injuries.

The under-reporting of accidents to young workers is borne out by the findings of surveys that questioned young people themselves.[2] About one-third of working young people in these surveys reported having had an accident while working. These studies provided few details about the nature and severity of injuries or the type of work they were associated with. However, the Birmingham study, *The Hidden Army*, gave information about the reported accidents and injuries.[3] One third of young people (30 per cent) said they had suffered an accident. Boys had twice as many accidents as girls. One-third of injuries (27 per cent) needed medical attention. Several of these injuries were serious, such as a girl who caught her hand in a machine and a boy who broke his leg when the jack holding up the car he was lying under gave way. Almost half (40 per cent) of young people working in cafés or restaurants had been involved in an accident, but only just over a third needed medical attention. While few young people working with animals had reported accidents (24 per cent), the majority of resulting injuries (80 per cent) needed medical attention. One-third of newspaper delivery boys and girls (36 per cent) had suffered an injury, including dog bites, falls from bicycles and trapping fingers in letter boxes.

PHYSICAL RISKS TO YOUNG WORKERS

Adolescence is a time of considerable physical change. Development at puberty is closely related to a growth spurt, but the timing of these physical changes differs considerably between individuals. Boys enter puberty about six months later than girls and they have a growth spurt at a later stage.[4] It is therefore extremely difficult to make general statements about what young people can physically cope with at different ages. However, there are four areas in which young people's health can be at risk. There is evidence that young people should not be expected to lift the same weights as adults. A study in the United States showed that young workers were more likely to have back injuries, in particular when they were physically small.[5] In the UK, Post Office guidelines on 'safe' weights for adult employees recommend a maximum of 15 kilos. The guideline for a 16-year-old trainee recommends a weight of 11.5 kilos. A report published by the World Health Organisation (WHO) argues that young people who are exposed to toxic chemicals at work may be more readily affected than adults by the same concentrations of these chemicals.[6] Similarly, young people seem to be more severely affected by exposure to noise and to extremes of heat and cold. This means that limits set for adults are not appropriate for young people.

Finally, young workers are known to tire more easily than adults. Fatigue can lead to lapses of concentration at work which can cause accidents.

YOUNG WORKERS' INCREASED RISKS OF ACCIDENTS

A recent report published by the Child Accident Prevention Trust has pointed out that young workers may be at greater risk of sustaining accidents at work than adults for a number of reasons.[7] Young workers' inexperience means that they are often unable to adequately judge whether the work they do could lead to injury. A study of young people in the United States aged between 14 and 16 who had suffered injuries at work requiring hospital treatment showed that almost half had not realised the work they did could lead to injuries.[8] Yet young workers are often required to realise the risk they run, for example, when working with heavy weights, machinery or sharp instruments. Even the traditional school student job of newspaper delivery requires a 'common sense' judgement of dangers associated with walking or cycling on main roads and travelling in the dark. If not properly instructed and supervised, young people may well fail to realise the potential dangers to their safety.

A number of studies have claimed that young people often take more risk than older people, but there was disagreement over whether this was due to inexperience or the developmental characteristics of puberty. For example, Concoran concluded that accidents to young farm workers using machinery were at least partly due to '...their youthful inexperience and exuberance'.[9] Bennett linked adolescents' risk-taking behaviour to hormonal changes in puberty which increase aggressiveness and impulsiveness.[10] Siegal *et al* attributed the tendency to risk-taking to rapid fluctuations in moods which are said to be characteristic of puberty.[11]

The specific nature of young workers' employment may also contribute to an increased risk of accidents. Compared to adults, the working situation of employees under the age of 16 is particularly insecure. They are employed on a part-time, often casual basis, they are not expected to stay in the job for very long and they often receive low wages. A survey of 200 workers aged between 12 and 18 who were still in full-time education found that their average rate of pay was about half that for adults.[12] Other studies found that young workers were paid on average £1.50 per hour, while some earned well below this rate.[13] There is no proven connection between low rates of pay, insecure working conditions and accidents. However, there is evidence that a lack of training and skills increases the risk of accidents. Many employers who regard young workers as a source of cheap and temporary labour are unlikely to invest time and effort in adequate safety training. Consequently, young people may be particularly at risk of accidents at work.

DO YOUNG WORKERS AND THEIR PARENTS WORRY ABOUT THEIR SAFETY?

As part of the study of young workers commissioned by the Child Accident Prevention Trust,[14] a small questionnaire survey examined young people's and their parents' attitudes to safety at work. The questionnaires (one for the young person and one for the parents) asked a series of questions about the nature of the job, whether in their opinion the job was safe, whether they would have liked more information about safety measures or supervision, and whether they had ever had an accident at work. The questionnaires were handed out by local authority education welfare officers in Bedfordshire, Lincolnshire, Norfolk and Suffolk to young people applying for work permits in both rural and urban areas. It should be emphasised that this is not a representative sample because all the young people were seeking work permits and were therefore likely to know at least something about the legislation governing the employment of young people. The survey did not include the views of parents and young people who did not know about or were not applying for permits. The numbers involved in the survey are too small to allow for specific conclusions to be drawn. Within the short period in which the survey was carried out (three months) 153 young people and their parents completed and returned the questionnaires. Nevertheless, the survey provides some insight into attitudes towards safety.

THE YOUNG PEOPLE

The young people responding to the questionnaire were aged between 13 and 15 years old. More boys than girls replied (62 per cent of the respondents were boys and 38 per cent girls), which may well reflect a larger number of boys working. Most of the young people delivered newspapers or free leaflets, while a minority worked in shops or catering. Other jobs included bunching flowers, packing boxes, gardening, life guarding, clerical work and cleaning (see Table 6.3).

TABLE 6.3 **Jobs of young workers responding to a questionnaire on safety at work**

Job	Number of young workers	% of all jobs
Paper delivery	91	60
Shop work	18	12
Catering	16	11
Other	28	17

The majority of young people (91 per cent) felt that their jobs were safe. Those who did feel worried about their safety at work mentioned the risk of dog bites, safety on the road, sexual harassment and being approached by strangers. However, a large proportion (77 per cent) felt that they were not given enough instructions on how to work safely, or none at all. Just over half (55 per cent) felt that they should be supervised when starting a job. More than half (68 per cent) felt confident enough to speak up for themselves if they were asked to do work which they thought might be dangerous to their health or could cause an accident.

Only eight young people (5 per cent) reported having had an accident at work, including dog bites, one road traffic accident and a back injury as a result of carrying a heavy bag of newspapers.

THE PARENTS

The majority of parents (75 per cent) were not worried about their children's safety at work. Comments made included: 'It's only a paper round'; 'My daughter is very sensible'; and 'I know the person my son works for.' A sizeable minority (25 per cent) were worried about safety at work. Concerns about safety were related to road traffic accidents, bad weather conditions, carrying heavy bags and attacks by dogs. Comments expressing worry included: 'I am worried about an accident on his bike'; 'I worry about dogs biting him'; and 'I would be worried if he had to do his paper round in an isolated area.'

The majority of parents (64 per cent) had taken responsibility for checking their children's working conditions by visiting the workplace or accompanying their children on their paper rounds. Several parents mentioned that they knew the employer personally and could rely on them to provide a safe working environment. Others, whose children were working for large, well-known companies, commented that they expected well-established firms to have adequate safety and training policies.

Most parents (84 per cent) said that they would stop their child from working if the job was dangerous to their health; if the job was affecting their school work; if they were exploited in terms of pay and working hours; if the job involved using dangerous machinery; if they were approached by a stranger during their paper rounds. Several parents said they would not interfere but leave the decision to the child, while one parent commented that the benefits of the job – a sense of achievement and self-worth – outweighed the possible dangers.

The survey showed that, while having a positive attitude towards work, young people and their parents are aware of potential dangers. The majority of parents had taken steps to check that the employment was safe and young people themselves were aware of the need for safety training and supervision. However, the survey did not investigate to what extent employers did provide training and supervision.

IS WORK GOOD FOR YOUNG PEOPLE?

The previously cited comment by a parent that the benefits of having a job outweigh the possible costs of injury is important. It may well reflect the attitude of many parents, other adults such as teachers and the young people themselves. It is easy to think of ways in which young people might benefit from doing paid work. Gaining independence and confidence, learning to accept responsibility and take initiative, learning new practical skills, learning the value of money earned – these are some positive aspects of work. However, research evidence backing up these positive common sense assumptions is scarce.

The notion that young people can only benefit from part-time work has been challenged by researchers in the United States, in particular through Greenberger and Steinberg's book, *When Teenagers Work: the psychological and social costs of adolescent employment*.[15] The authors emphasised that it is necessary to balance social approval of young people's working by recognising that there may be a negative side to it. Using research based on representative samples of young workers, they set out to demonstrate that, far from being nothing but 'healthy', work can potentially be harmful to young people. The main message put across by Greenberger and Steinberg was that the kinds of jobs taken on by young people may not encourage a sense of responsibility or commitment. As they put it, 'Jobs that are impersonal, temporary, offer few opportunities for advancement and don't lead to desirable future employment elicit – at best – dependable but not extraordinary performance from employees'.[16] The authors were also sceptical about the opportunity for young workers to learn new skills on the job. The majority of jobs held by young workers, they argued, required basic skills they did not need to learn, such as sweeping floors, unloading boxes or stacking shelves.

Previous research carried out by the same authors identified two reasons why work might be stressful for young people.[17] First, young people already invest a considerable amount of time in school work, homework, leisure activities, peer relationships and family commitments (helping with household chores). The addition of extensive working hours, they argued, could cause considerable stress, leading to behaviour and health problems. Second, the conditions that often characterise their jobs may well be particularly stressful to young people. These include exposure to excessive heat or noise; tasks that young people find boring and repetitive; a lack of influence on decisions about what to do and how to do it; and being paid low wages. Greenberger and Steinberg also suggest a link between the hours children work and alcohol consumption;[18] subsequent studies by the same researchers confirmed this evidence.[19] However, the reasons for this link are not certain, and there have been no studies in the UK to support or refute these findings. Greenberger and Steinberg have also suggested that the negative aspects of part-time employment might have long-term effects.[20] After having had a succession of unskilled, boring and poorly paid jobs, they claim, young workers can become disillusioned. Instead of gaining an appetite for work, some young people became cynical and were unable to regard work as an enjoyable experience.

While highlighting the negative aspects of work, Greenberger and Steinberg also identified some positive features. They acknowledged the value of feeling less financially dependent on parents and having the freedom to do what they wanted with their earned money. Yet, even this experience was not considered wholly positive. Work, Greenberger and Steinberg argued, becomes associated with earning money and can encourage an excessively material attitude. The most positive effect of work, as identified by Greenberger and his colleagues, was an improvement in interpersonal relationships. They found that, compared with peers who did not have a job, young workers had a greater understanding of social relationships and were better able to relate to other people's points of view.[21]

The rather pessimistic picture painted by Greenberger and Steinberg has been challenged by another researcher. Using interviews with high school students in the United States as the basis of his research, Green argued that part-time employment while still in full-time education can serve a number of positive functions, including facilitating the transition from school to work and offering young people the opportunity to gain wider social experience outside school and family.[22] Contrary to Greenberger and Steinberg, he emphasised the active role played by young workers themselves. He claimed that the young people he interviewed showed a positive attitude to work which is valuable in itself and should be recognised. He also stressed that, far from being passive 'victims' of their jobs, young people changed their employment or reduced their working times when they saw it as negatively affecting them or as interfering with other interests, including school work.

Green's findings have been replicated in the UK by McKechnie et al.[23] The researchers interviewed 56 secondary school students aged between 12 and 16. The interviews covered the level of responsibility in the workplace, contact with adults through their jobs and the extent to which they could make decisions regarding the work they were doing. The results provided some support for Green's argument for a more positive stance. However, McKechnie et al warned against over-generalisation. They argued that Green failed to consider the importance of the type of job young workers have. The demands and opportunities provided by different jobs can vary widely and it is too simplistic to assume that all jobs offer the same possibilities to develop social skills. The young workers they interviewed reported considerable variations in terms of the level of interaction with adults, the perceived value of the job, the amount of independence or participation in decision-making offered and their perceived role in the workplace. They also pointed out that few of the young workers had the power to change their working conditions. When dissatisfied with the conditions of their job, the only option open to them was to leave. However, like Green, McKechnie *et al* found that young people regard part-time employment as preparing them for the adult world of work and hoped it would help them find a future job.

THE EFFECT OF WORK ON EDUCATION

The effect of work on young people's academic achievements has received considerable attention in recent years. In the United States, the interest in the link between schooling and work was based on concern that part-time employment could stretch young people's psychological and physical resources to the point where their academic achievement suffered. Initially, Greenberger and Steinberg reported that young workers did less well academically than their non-working peers.[24] However, subsequent research reported a more detailed effect which was less pessimistic. Steinberg *et al* closely examined the characteristics of almost 2,000 school students, before and after they took up part-time work.[25] They found that young people who spent a considerable amount of time working (more than 20 hours per week) were less interested in school and did less well academically than their peers who did not work, even before they took on a job. While their lack of interest in school may have contributed to their decision to work long hours, it made a bad situation worse because it led to poor school attendance and a failure to do homework. On the other hand, students who worked a moderate number of hours were doing as well academically as those who did not work. The researchers concluded that the number of hours worked are crucial in whether or not paid employment has a negative effect on educational achievement.

Studies carried out in this country similarly suggested that young people who work moderate hours do academically as well or better than their non-working classmates, while those working long hours tend to do significantly worse.[26]

CONCLUSIONS

The findings of research discussed in previous sections have not provided a clear answer to the question of whether work is healthy or harmful to young people. Although the initial reports published by researchers in the United States have been largely negative and over-pessimistic, they helped to put work in perspective and counter-balance commonsense notions that employment of young people still in full-time education can only be good for them. In particular, the studies pointed out that the nature of the jobs held by the majority of young people limits the psychological benefits in terms of gaining a sense of self-confidence and independence. However, as more recent studies have pointed out, over-generalisation ignores the variation in young workers' experiences. While many jobs open to young people are of low status and low pay, they may still offer opportunities for stimulation and learning. Even so-called boring and repetitive jobs may, from the young people's perspective, be worth while, albeit not in every respect. What is lacking in the current research available is the views of young workers themselves and their perspective of the good and bad aspects of their jobs.

One issue which needs more attention is the possibility of accidents at work. Adequate information on the extent of accidents and the types of jobs associated with accidents is scant enough for adults, but even less is known about the extent of accidents to young people or the types of jobs that put them at risk. The social context of young workers' jobs as well as their particular adolescent physical and psychological characteristics may well put them at greater risk of accidents. If this increased risk is not widely recognised by employers and acted upon, young workers may not be adequately protected against accidents. The small-scale survey carried out by the Child Accident Prevention Trust[27] showed that, while young people and their parents are generally aware of possible dangers, they tend to rely on employers to provide adequate protection. Research into employers' attitudes towards young workers and employers' safety practices is needed to establish whether young workers' and parents' faith in them is justified.

NOTES

1   S Hobbs and J McKechnie, *Child Employment in Britain: A social and*

psychological analysis, Stationery Office, 1997.

2 C Pond and A Searle, *The Hidden Army: children at work in the 1990s*, Low Pay Unit, 1991; S Hobbs, S Lindsay and J McKechnie, *Children at work: part-time employment in North Tyneside*, A report to North Tyneside Council, University of Paisley, 1993; S Hobbs, S Lindsay and J McKechnie, 'Part-time employment and academic achievement', *Scottish Educational Review*, 25, 1993, pp53–60; J McKechnie, S Lindsay and S Hobbs, *Child employment in Cumbria*, A report to Cumbria County Council, University of Paisley, 1993; J McKechnie, S Lindsay and S Hobbs, *Still Forgotten: child employment in Dumfries and Galloway*, Scottish Low Pay Unit, 1994; F Joliffe, S Patel, Y Sparks and K Reardon, *Child Employment in Greenwich*, London Borough of Greenwich, 1995.

3 Pond and Searle, *ibid*.

4 E C Crowne and D B Dunger, 'Growth and Puberty' in A McFarlane (ed), *Adolescent Medicine*, Royal College of Physicians, 1996.

5 D L Parker, W R Carl, L R French and F B Martin, 'Characteristics of adolescent work injuries reported to the Minnesota Department of Labor and Industry', *American Journal of Public Health*, 8, 1994, pp606–611.

6 World Health Organisation, *Children at Work: special health risks – Report of a WHO Study Group*, WHO Technical Report Series 756, WHO, 1987.

7 E Heptinstall, K Jewitt and C Sherriff, *Young Workers and their Accidents*, Child Accident Prevention Trust, 1997.

8 E B Knight, D N Castillo and L A Layne, 'A detailed analysis of work-related injury among youth treated in emergency departments', *American Journal of Industrial Medicine*, 27, 1995, pp793–805.

9 H Corcoran, 'Safety of Youths in Agriculture', *Safety Standards*, 16, 1967, pp1–3.

10 D L Bennett, *Adolescent Health in Australia: an overview of needs and approaches to care – A Health Promotion Mongraph*, Australian Medical Association, 1984.

11 W A Siegal, P Cuccaro, J T Parsons, J Wall and A D Weinberg, 'Adolescents thinking about emotions and risk taking' in J Puckett and H W Reese (eds), *Mechanisms of Everyday Cognition*, Lawrence Erlbaum & Associates, 1993.

12 GMB Union, *Part-time work among school pupils and college students under age 19*, GMB, 1995.

13 Pond and Searle, *op cit*; Hobbs *et al*, *op cit*.

14 Heptinstall *et al*, *op cit*.

15 E Greenberger and L Steinberg, *When Teenagers Work: The psychological and social costs of adolescent employment*, New York, Basic Books, 1986.

16 *Ibid*, p99.

17 E Greenberger, L Steinberg and A Vaux, 'Adolescents who work: health and behavioral consequences of job stress', *Developmental Psychology*, 17, 1981, pp691-703.

18 Greenberger and Steinberg, *op cit.*

19 L Steinberg, S Fegley and S M Dorenbusch, 'Negative impact of part-time work on adolescent adjustment: Evidence from a longitudinal study', *Developmental Psychology*, 29, 1993, pp171-180.

20 Greenberger and Steinberg, *op cit.*

21 L Steinberg, E Greenberger, M Jacobi and L Garduque, 'Early work experience: a partial anti-dote for adolescent egocentrism', *Journal of Youth and Adolescence*, 10, 1981, pp141-157.

22 D Green, 'High school student employment in social context: adolescents' perceptions of the role of part-time work', *Adolescence*, 225, 1990, pp425-435.

23 J McKechnie, S Lindsay, S Hobbs and M Lavalette, 'Adolescents' perception of the role of part-time work', *Adolescence*, 31, 1996, pp193-204.

24 Greenberger and Steinberg, *op cit.*

25 Steinberg *et al*, 1993, *op cit.*

26 Hobbs *et al*, *op cit*; J McKechnie, S Hobbs and S Lindsay, *Educational impact of part-time employment on school pupils: A report to the Scottish Office Education Department*, University of Paisley, 1995.

27 Heptinstall *et al*, *op cit.*

7 Work experience or experience of work?*

INTRODUCTION
BRIDGET PETTITT

As previous chapters clearly show, many children in the UK combine part-time, paid work with full-time education. Many children have experienced different types of work by the time they leave school. Schools and the education system as a whole have long recognised the value of 'work' as part of mainstream education but, despite this, have paid little attention to the educational aspect of children's part-time employment. The work-based curriculum, including work experience programmes, has largely developed without taking into account the work that children may already be doing. Indeed, the focus of research and policy from an educational point of view has been the (mainly negative) impact of children's part-time work on their education. These issues are explored in detail in Chapter 6, and are not revisited here.

This chapter attempts to draw together analysis of children's experience of work in the two areas: school-based, work-related curriculums, and 'naturally occurring' part-time work which children have chosen to do outside the school environment. It focuses on the skills and experience that children may draw from both situations. First, the role of school-based work experience is discussed by

---

* Case studies by *Norman Barton and Shirley Horton, Peele School, Lincolnshire* and by *Jim McKechnie, Sandy Hobbs and Sandra Lindsay, Department of Applied Social Studies, University of Paisley, with contributions from Bridget Pettitt.*

Norman Barton and Shirley Horton. Secondly, Jim McKechnie, Sandy Hobbs and Sandra Lindsay analyse some new data on the different jobs children do at different stages in their schooling. A career path in part-time work as they progress through school emerges.

SCHOOL-BASED WORK EXPERIENCE SCHEMES

The education system and schools themselves have long acknowledged the importance of work-related elements in the school curriculum. Schools integrate elements of the world of work in various ways within the curriculum. It can take the form of specific vocational courses such as business studies, elements of business or industry integrated into subject work, research projects based in a work situation, and work experience placements where school students spend a certain amount of time in a work environment. It is available to all 14 to 16-year-olds in state education.

In a recent review of the 'work-related curriculum' it can be seen that such provision has four objectives:

- to provide knowledge and understanding of the world of work;
- to develop key skills such as communication and team working;
- to affect the students motivation by relating education to the world of work;
- to allow them to effectively plan post-16 routes relating to training and further education.[1]

The following case study is an example of a work experience scheme in a school. It outlines the background and aims of the work placements in this particular school and the way they are established. It then goes on to provide some feedback on the impact of the scheme for employers, pupils, their parents and the school.

WORK EXPERIENCE AT PEELE SCHOOL – A CASE STUDY
NORMAN BARTON AND SHIRLEY HORTON

The Peele school is a small secondary school of 350 pupils catering for the 11–16 age range in Long Sutton, Lincolnshire. Approximately 35 per cent of children in the area are selected to attend local grammar schools. The area is isolated, the town itself surrounded by arable farms and market gardens. Unemployment is not high, but it is predominantly a low wage area. The main employers are the farms and market gardens referred to above, as well as industries such as food processing and transport.

Work experience has been in place at the school since the early 1970s when the school leaving age was raised. At the time it was introduced, pupils aged 15–16 were given one day a week in a chosen workplace to gain real experience of the world of work and to learn skills they would need for their future employment. The intention was also to increase each pupil's chances of finding permanent employment.

The school believes that this early enterprise succeeded. Large numbers of pupils did find jobs through their work experience and we know of several who are still there today. Local employers rapidly gained confidence in the scheme and soon learned that this was an opportunity for them to recruit their future workforce.

Since those early beginnings the scheme has changed. It now involves 15 and 16-year-old pupils who are placed with an employer for 10 days. The work they do is unpaid. In today's world where qualifications are increasingly important, we no longer allocate 20 per cent of the timetable to the scheme. It is now seen as an integral part of the Key Stage 4[2] curriculum and is linked directly to GCSE and GNVQ work in school. The intention is no longer to assume that the work placement will lead to permanent employment, although that does happen. We expect pupils to broaden their horizons, to see what career possibilities exist and evaluate them realistically. We encourage more and more of our pupils to continue in education beyond 16 years and to have further experiences of work before deciding what to commit themselves to. Above all we encourage our pupils to develop as many skills as possible so that they become more employable rather than looking for one job at 16 which will be for life.

Some of the aims of work experience related to the pupils are:

- to develop their personal and social skills through working with adults in a working environment;
- to develop self-awareness and raise self-esteem;
- to understand the world of work and how a workplace operates;
- to apply or learn about the application of skills and knowledge learned in the school curriculum;
- to understand some of the rights, responsibilities and obligations

associated with work;
- to help pupils to develop career ideas through actual working experience;
- to raise pupil aspirations and develop the concept of the need for qualifications and lifelong learning;
- to realise their strengths and weaknesses and to develop necessary skills.

Preparation for work experience begins early. From 11 years old, pupils are gaining awareness of the sorts of employment available locally. In geography they study the local environment and economy and soon understand the local employment structure. In science and technology pupils gain an understanding of the processes used in local agricultural and processing industries. At 13 or 14 years, pupils are given advice about course options and career choices, and in the spring term they spend one day with a local employer. The main aims of this 'work shadowing' experience are to build confidence and to develop communication skills, especially with adults. With this comes a heightened awareness of local industry, of the work that goes on, of the products made, and of the importance of trade and links with Europe and the rest of the world. We also hope that they develop an understanding of how the curriculum in school links with the world of work.

We find that many 14-year-olds have a romanticised view of the job they think they would like to do. Work shadowing can be a very important first step in correcting this. Each year there are a number of aspiring hairdressers, boys and girls, who have a vision of a glamorous career. A day spent in a busy salon can show them that there are many other aspects of the work which lessen the glamour. Hours of standing, cleaning the floor, washing towels and making drinks for clients and colleagues give a different perspective to starry-eyed potential Vidal Sassoons.

The work shadowing experience also helps pupils to make informed choices for their work experience placement 18 months later. Many choose to return to the same employer and some are invited back by the employer because of the positive impression they have made. For some, however, the shadowing experience leads to big changes in areas of interest. They learn rapidly from the first experience that this is not for them and they are keen to try something else.

At about this time pupils are also being asked to make choices for subjects to be studied in Key Stage 4. As well as advice given by form tutors, careers advisers and teachers, pupils can draw on the knowledge they have gained from their shadowing experience to make more informed subject choices for GCSE and GNVQ courses.

Planning for work experience begins when they are 14 or 15 years old; form tutors and the careers co-ordinator work with pupils and parents to identify appropriate placements. We provide a wide variety of work placements – for example, animal care, nursing, engineering computing, work in the theatre, with local primary schools, accountancy and retailing. Some employment placements are prohibited – for example, working in scrap yards, fish frying or any work involving dangerous equipment such as meat slicers or guillotines. We discourage pupils from seeking placements with family and friends wherever possible so that new experiences can be gained.

For some pupils we actively search out what we refer to as 'sheltered' placements where we know the employer will be sympathetic and understanding towards a pupil who may have learning difficulties. Our main aim is to develop confidence and to help the pupil to gain the experience of working with adults, often for the first time, and to understand the importance of good time-keeping. The careers co-ordinator visits the employer with the pupil to discuss individual needs before the placement is made.

When contact has been made with likely employers, pupils are encouraged to write formal application letters for a work experience placement. A significant number of employers respond to these letters and agree to interview the applicant. Preparing for the interview is very important – issues like dress code and how to get there by a certain time become real. Employers also give feedback, and what had previously been seen as a piece of school work suddenly becomes real and relevant.

The careers co-ordinator monitors the programme, making sure each employer is aware of her/his responsibilities. We have to be sure that the employer understands the aims of the placement as well as providing evidence that a risk assessment has been carried out. We insist on knowing what each pupil is going to do before the placement begins and reject some placements where the plan does not meet the pupil's needs.

The scheme demands a great deal from employers, the pupils themselves, and from careers staff, form tutors and parents. We have found that it brings benefits to all parties involved.

EMPLOYERS' PERSPECTIVE

Each year employers complete a report and assessment of the pupil. On the whole they have found the experience very worthwhile. They sometimes seem surprised that the young people have real skills, are personable, co-operative and polite. They discover that the pupils are ambitious and want to make every effort to succeed in their placement.

He has done everything they have asked of him and has fitted in well with everyone ... He has a very positive attitude to work.

She was well-organised, adaptable and willing to undertake any activity using her own initiative.

He has mixed well with all the staff ... and has completed all given tasks without problems.

PARENTS' PERSPECTIVE

From the outset parents have a part to play in explaining the purpose of the placement and, for some pupils, helping them to overcome their fear and trepidation. At the end parents are invited to comment on the usefulness of the exercise – on the effects it might have had on their child's self-confidence and attitudes to school, and on their future career. Usually they are very positive and can see easily identifiable changes in character and behaviour.

For example:

He was nervous the first morning but he soon got over that and enjoyed every morning after. It has given him confidence to communicate with adults ... and an insight into what will be expected from him when he finally goes into employment ... I believe it is a good experience for all kids to do, to show them what working life is like, to help them make up their minds for the future.

It has helped to build up her self-confidence...

Having attended the interview with Steven ... I felt that the programme of learning they had arranged... would be beneficial in allowing him to try a variety of employment opportunities in the hospitality field ... This experience has allowed him to expand his knowledge of a workplace environment ... His priority is to achieve good grades in his coming GCSE exams which will allow him greater choice in future careers.

Most parents are very supportive of the scheme. They see a link between the work experience and more enthusiastic attitudes to school work. The experience also helps children to see their parents in a different light and to understand the demands of working day in day out.

She now understands why I am so tired at night ... Working is hard.

Sometimes parents can be negative and a very small number each year see work experience as an opportunity to enhance the family's income. A few parents are therefore resentful that the work is unpaid.

SCHOOL'S PERSPECTIVE

In terms of the school it enhances the curriculum, giving it more meaning and relevance to the world of work. In broadens the school experience and allows children to see and use equipment that we cannot afford in school. Teachers certainly gain from the experience. All pupils are visited at least twice. It is demanding and time consuming but it helps the school to develop links in the local business community. It helps teachers keep in touch with requirements outside the school environment. The English Department in school links very closely with the work experience programme. Pupils learn how to write letters to prospective employers, and are given practice in interview and telephone techniques. A very important part of the experience is to keep a daily diary and this is used as part of the English GCSE course to produce a written report. Some pupils also use their diary as the basis for an oral presentation, another component of the GCSE course.

There are many other areas of the curriculum where such links could be made. For example, planning the design and preparation of a variety of cakes is an integral part of the food technology course. We have visited pupils working in the local bakers and have suggested that this project could be linked to a work experience placement.

CHILDREN'S PERSPECTIVE

The biggest gainers are the pupils. For some they feel successful for the first time. They find employers who treat them as equals and give them responsibility. They feel valued. Although the school tries to treat pupils in the same way, it seems the work experience succeeds where school efforts have failed.

Pupils learn about the routine of going to work. They need to travel quite long distances and the length of the working day sometimes comes as a surprise. At the end of a day many are tired. Many begin to sort out their ideas for future education, and set targets for their final school year. Many realise the importance of aiming higher than they might previously have done to escape the more mundane jobs they have seen on their placement. Communication skills improve. They meet unfamiliar adults, they answer the telephone and quickly learn the correct way to address people in the work environment. They develop skills learned in school and bring back new skills. Employers are only too willing to act as referees for college or for potential employers. Sometimes employers offer employment or apprenticeships. Pupils learn the importance of doing quality work, of working to tight schedules and of becoming a team member. They learn to use their initiative – to see jobs which need doing and not wait to be told to do them. They learn commitment and self discipline.

We cannot pretend that pupils' attitudes to school work are completely transformed by the fortnight's experience. However, for some, aspirations are raised. They understand from people who are not their teachers or parents that school work and success in public examinations are linked. Some realise that while mundane and unskilled jobs pay well in the eyes of a 16-year-old, they lead to a life of low pay and a high risk of unemployment. These pupils return to school with a new determination to do well and with new aspirations. Many pupils seem more mature, more purposeful and more determined.

THE VALUE OF WORK EXPERIENCE

The above case study shows the advantages that school age children can gain from being placed in a work environment for a short period of time. They learn about the world of work, acquire skills such as communicating, and gain in confidence and understanding. Many of these gains can also be seen in the responses made by children in part-time work elsewhere in this volume (see particularly Chapter 4). However, attitudes towards work experience schemes and children doing part-time paid employment are very different. Whereas work experience is seen as a valuable and integral part of education, part-time working is often seen as in direct conflict. One of the reasons may be that work placements are carefully chosen to maximise the learning process and to ensure that pupils are developing and using new skills.

Given that the type of job and working environment is crucial in work experience programmes, it is important to establish what types of jobs children do in part-time work. Do they provide the opportunity to learn the kinds of skills that are valued in the work placement settings? Do children progress on to other jobs as they get older and acquire more skills? The following study traces the different part-time jobs children do as they progress through school, by comparing the jobs done by younger and older school students. This begins to give us an idea of the types of work experience children may get in 'naturally occurring' work outside education.

WORK AND THE OLDER SCHOOL STUDENT
JIM MCKECHNIE , SANDY HOBBS AND SANDRA LINDSAY

The extent to which school students in Britain combine full-time education with part-time work has been attracting increasing attention. A recent review of studies of the extent of this pheno-menon concluded that the majority of pupils will have some experience of paid employment before reaching the minimum school leaving age.[3] There is evidence that they will have worked in a wide range of jobs beyond the stereotyped notion of 'children's jobs' such as newspaper delivery, and that most of the work is undertaken illegally.[4]

The focus of most of the research has been on school students under 16 years of age. Less attention has been paid to those who remain in full-time education after the minimum school leaving age. A small number of studies do exist which indicate that in the later years of school, students continue to combine full-time study with part-time employment. For example, Tymms and Fitz-Gibbon found that 50 per cent of students in the first and second year of A-level study were working.[5] On average they were working nine hours per week, with 10 per cent working in excess of 20 hours per week.

The level of employment found by Tymms and Fitz-Gibbon is less than that found in other studies.[6] Micklewright, Rajah and Smith employed data from the Family Expenditure Survey covering the period 1968-91.[7] Their analysis showed that in the 1968-71 period, 40 per cent of 16–18-year-olds who remained in full-time education had part-time jobs. This rose to 59 per cent in the 1988-91 period. It appears that, not only is this age group combining work and schooling, but the trend is for the numbers working to increase over time. There are a number of gaps in our knowledge. For example, are older age groups involved in the same forms of work as the younger pupils who have been more fully studied?

Based on research in the United States, Mortimer and Finch argue that part-time employment may be beneficial to individual development and may lead to the attainment of a number of skills.[8] They also warn that we should not look at school students' jobs through adult eyes. Many of the types of jobs done by school students would appear boring and mundane to adults but from the perspective of the adolescent may be challenging and interesting. In one study of school students' work in the United States, the authors claimed that it was possible to identify a progression in the types of jobs being done.[9] A form of 'career path' emerged where younger pupils were employed in less demanding forms of work but, as they got older, entered more demanding employment. These more demanding forms of work have greater potential to lead to the development of useful skills and abilities.

With the aid of financial support from the Nuffield Foundation,[10] we undertook a small-scale study of this issue, because no equivalent British study appeared to exist. Our investigation compared school students above and below the minimum school leaving age, in order to explore the possibility, in a British context, of identifying a progression in the forms of employment which school students undertake. We also looked at the number of hours working students committed to their employment.

THE STUDY

The data was collected from three schools in urban Scotland, which were similar in terms of size and socio-economic factors. Information was gathered on the nature of the students' work history, including current and previous employment, types of job, rates of pay and hours worked. In addition, students were asked about accidental injury, start and finish times, and the perceived impact of their work on attendance, but the present analysis focuses upon the former set of information. Work is defined as naturally occurring paid employment outside of the family.[11] The exclusion of employment within the family is not meant to diminish its potential importance, but to acknowledge that this form of work is worthy of separate study.

Questionnaires were administered to students in three school years – 3rd (aged 14–15), 5th (aged 16–17) and 6th (aged 17–18). To ensure comparability, standard guidelines were used by all data collectors and the researchers were on hand to answer any questions that arose.

Table 7.1 provides a breakdown of sample sizes in each school and completion rates. While completion rates are high, it should be noted that employment may be related to poor attendance.[12] It is therefore possible that, if there is a higher incidence of work among absentees, the present estimate of numbers working is an underestimate.

TABLE 7.1 **Sample sizes and completion rates**

	No. of students	Completed no	%
3rd year	561	475	85
5th year	443	345	78
6th year	228	164	72
Total	1,232	984	80

The students were classified as either current workers (working at the time of the study), former workers (not working at time of the study but had been employed in the past), or never worked. Table 7.2 shows the percentage of students within each category.

TABLE 7.2 **Work status (percentages)**

	Current worker	Former worker	Never worked
3rd year	33	25	43
5th year	41	22	37
6th year	57	14	29

Students in later years were more likely to be currently working and less likely to have never worked by the time they reached 6th year. The pattern was not identical for each individual school, which may reflect different local economic circumstances or may indicate a conscious decision by 5th year pupils in one school not to work. The end of the 5th year in Scottish schools is when students face their 'Highers', an important set of examinations.

When boys' and girls' employment levels are considered separately (see Table 7.3), we discover that the trend towards a greater extent of employment in later years is largely due to the female students. Variations between the three year groups were significant for females, but not for males.

TABLE 7.3 **Work status: male and female (percentages)**

		Current worker	Former worker	Never worked	N
3rd year	Male	32	30	38	250 (100%)
	Female	33	20	47	225 (100%)
5th year	Male	37	27	36	162 (100%)
	Female	44	19	37	183 (100%)
6th year	Male	44	17	39	66 (100%)
	Female	65	12	22	98 (100%)

Table 7.4 provides a breakdown of the forms of employment by category. Analysis of this data showed 3rd years were more likely to be employed in delivery, babysitting and hawking jobs. In contrast, 5th and 6th year students were more likely to be employed in shop work, hotel and catering and 'other' forms of employment. No variation from this pattern was found within any of the individual schools. The 'other' category of job type included hairdressing, cleaning, manual labouring, garage, secretarial, telephone and care work.

TABLE 7.4 **Job type (percentages)**

	3rd year	5th year	6th year
Delivery	56	29	5
Hawking	8	3	3
Shop work	7	29	47
Babysitting	16	9	5
Waiting	3	5	5
Hotel/catering	3	11	16
Other	8	15	18
	100	100	100

In the 3rd year, male employment is dominated by delivery work and this drops significantly in the 6th year to be replaced by shop work, hotel/catering and 'other' types of jobs. For females, 3rd years are employed in babysitting and hawking jobs. Among the older female students shop work, waiting and hotel/catering work dominate (see Table 7.5).

TABLE 7.5 **Job type: male and female (percentages)**

	3rd year		5th year		6th year	
	M	F	M	F	M	F
Delivery	86	24	56	9	10	3
Hawking	4	13	3	3	–	5
Shop work	4	9	14	40	50	45
Babysitting	–	32	2	14	–	8
Waiting	–	7	–	9	–	8
Hotel/catering	–	5	9	14	17	16
Other	6	11	17	14	23	16
	100	100	100	100	100	100

This tends to suggest that the main gender differences in types of jobs done between males and females is found in the earlier years. However, we need to be cautious in adopting this view since our data does not allow us to differentiate between the tasks done in any specific job category. Many older students are employed in shop work, but it may be that while the males tend to be shelf stackers, the females tend to be checkout operators.

Table 7.6 compares the hours worked per week and rates of pay in each of the school years. Students in 5th and 6th years are working longer hours on average, are paid higher rates and earn more per week. Note particularly that they are more likely to be committing 10 hours or more to their part-time job.

TABLE 7.6 **Hours worked and pay rates**

| | | | | Hours | Average Pay | |
| | | | | Percentages | | |
	5 or less	6 to 10	Over 10	Mean hours	Per hour	Per week
3rd year	51	39	10	6.3	£2.25	£13.44
5th year	31	36	33	9.1	£2.91	£23.51
6th year	21	42	38	10.8	£2.92	£28.62

No significant gender differences were found in hours worked, but males had significantly higher hourly rates of pay (£3.03) compared to females (£2.53).

The data does not allow us to say with confidence why so many older school students have jobs. Certainly wages averaging between £20 and £30 per week can be seen as a substantial contribution to family income. What we may confidently say is that the results do show that 5th and 6th level students do work even though these are important examination years. We need to be cautious here. Since this data was not based on a longitudinal study, we cannot trace the work patterns of individuals. It is possible that some of this group of students leave work as examinations approach.

THE IMPACT OF WORK ON EDUCATION

Davies was among the first to draw attention to the negative association between work and education.[13] McKechnie et al found that those 15-year-olds working 10 hours or more per week were likely to have poorer grades and attendance.[14] The present study found that 38 per cent of 6th year students who were currently employed worked more than 10 hours per week. Two points need to be noted. It may not be the case that the same association exists for post-16-year-olds. Tymms and Fitz-Gibbon found that the amount of work done was not related to homework levels or A-level grades.[15] The analysis of Dustmann, Micklewright, Rajah and Smith, on the other hand, indicated a negative impact of work on educational performance.[16] They suggest that the effect may be related to the number of hours worked.

Even if a link is shown, the issue of causality is not yet clear. It is possible that working longer hours interferes with school performance, but alternatively it may be that those students doing less well educationally become less committed to school and spend more time working.

But what of the potential beneficial features of work? Mortimer *et al* suggest that in the United States there is typically a 'progression' in job types as students move through school.[17] The later years of school are marked by students working in more demanding forms of employment. Our data provides some support for this being the case in Britain. In general, students in the lower year were more likely to work in delivery and babysitting categories. The percentage employed in these categories drops significantly in the 6th year group with most working students employed in shop work, hotel and catering and the 'other' category, which are mainly adult forms of work, such as cleaner, secretary, telephonist.

The forms of employment which dominate amongst the older school students may have the potential to develop a range of skills for those who participate in them. The skills which Saunders *et al* associate with work experience programmes, such as communication skills and gaining a knowledge of the world of work, could be attained through such employment.[18] We do not know at present whether this is actually the case. However, at the very least it can be argued that the demands made by these jobs differ from the traditional newspaper delivery type of job and merit fuller consideration.

Consideration of job type also draws attention to variations between the sexes in this area. While the data shows that students in later years are more likely to work than those in earlier years, the change appears to be greatest for females. As we have seen, although in the 3rd year roughly equal percentages of males and females were working, in the 6th year proportionately more females than males were currently working. It is possible that as they get older female students are more interested in part-time work. In that sense the variations would be explained by suggesting 'supply side' differences.

However, it may also be the case that 'demand side' factors could explain the results. It is possible that in the later school years the types of businesses which are employing students wish to employ females rather than males. The level of demand for females in the retail sales and hotel and catering sectors, where 6th year school students are most likely to work, may be greater. More detailed study of the relationship between gender and part-time employment among this population is required.

Similarly, further research is required to ascertain whether the tasks carried out by employed students provide the potential for skill attainment discussed above. The study also suggests the need to reconsider the notion of 'work experience'. At present this concept appears to be closely tied to work placements organised by schools. All of the research suggests that most of the students who participate in work experience programmes will have employment experience from part-time jobs that they have found for themselves. Given this fact, there is a need to evaluate the contribution that such employment makes to the students' awareness of, and entry into, the world of work.

Saunders *et al* have clearly shown that there is a need to objectively evaluate the role, and the impact, of work experience programmes.[19] In our view it is also necessary to evaluate the extent to which children's 'real', everyday jobs contribute to their education and understanding of the world of work.

CONCLUSION
BRIDGET PETTITT

This chapter has brought together two studies on children's experiences of work in two separate contexts.

By drawing together these two perspectives, it is clear that there is an argument for bringing children's work experience in a school context and their part-time work outside school together. An analysis of the skills acquired by children in part-time jobs, in the same way as is being developed with work placements, would help move on the debate about what is acceptable or unacceptable employment for children. Schools could go further in recognising the achievements and skills gained by children who are working part time, and integrate this 'real world' experience into their school work in the same way as they integrate work placements.

NOTES

1 L Saunders, S Stoney and P Weston, 'The impact of the work-related curriculum on 14- to 16-year-olds', *Journal of Education and Work*, 10, 1997, pp151-167.

2 When examination courses begin – the last two years of compulsory education.

3 S Hobbs, S Lindsay and J McKechnie, 'The extent of child employment in Britain', *British Journal of Education and Work*, 9, 1996, pp5-18.

4 S Hobbs and J McKechnie, *Child Employment in Britain: A social and psychological analysis*, Stationery Office, 1997.

5 P B Tymms and C T Fitz-Gibbon, 'The relationship between part-time employment and A-level results', *Educational Research*, 34, 1992, pp193-199.

6 For example, Hutson and Cheung, 1990, cited in G Rikowski, *Working for Leisure? Part-time and Temporary Working among A-Level and BTEC National Students at Epping Forest College, A Report to Epping Forest College*, University of Birmingham, 1993.

7 J Micklewright, N Rajah and S Smith, 'Labouring and learning: part-time work and full-time education', *National Institute Economic Review*, 148, 1994, pp73-87.

8 J T Mortimer and M D Finch, *Adolescents, Work and Family: An Intergenerational Developmental Analysis*, California, Sage, 1996.

9 J T Mortimer, M D Finch, K Dennehy, T Lee and C Beebe, 'Work experience in adolescence', *Journal of Vocational Education Research*, 19, 1994, pp39-70.

10 This research was supported by a grant from the Nuffield Foundation under their Small Grants for the Social Sciences scheme, SOC/100(1438).

11 See E Greenberger and L Steinberg, *When Teenagers Work: The psychological and social costs of adolescent employment*, New York, Basic Books, 1986.

12 J McKechnie, S Lindsay and S Hobbs, 'Educational impact of part-time employment on school pupils', *British Psychological Society, Developmental Section*, 1995, University of Strathclyde: published in Proceedings of The British Psychological Society, 4, 2, 1996.

13 E Davies, 'Work out of school', *Education*, 10 November 1972, i-iv.

14 McKechnie *et al*, see note 12.

15 Tymms and Fitz-Gibbon, *op cit*.

16 C Dustmann, J Micklewright, N Rajah and S Smith, 'Earning and learning: Educational policy and the growth of part-time work by full-time pupils', *Fiscal Studies*, 17, 1996, pp79-103.

17 Mortimer *et al*, see note 9.

18 Saunders *et al*, see note 1.

19 *Ibid*.

Involving children and young people in policy and action: learning from international experiences

8

Rachel Marcus

INTRODUCTION

It is widely accepted that the main reason children work in the South*
is poverty;[1] in the UK the links between poverty and children
working are rather less clear.[2] The unattractiveness of poor quality,
irrelevant education compared with learning a skill through working
is another important factor in parts of the South. In the UK, by
contrast, however unattractive school is to some children, the
enforcement of education law means that very few children are
working full time during school hours. There are also common
aspects of child labour in both contexts. While work is beneficial to
some children and young people, the health or education of others is
jeopardised by working long hours in unsafe conditions in the UK as
well as in Southern countries. Worldwide, children and young people
are often paid much less than adults for similar work. In the UK, as in
many other countries, legislation has been ineffective in protecting
many working children from hazard and exploitation.[3]

Much action on child labour in the South aims to address poverty
and thereby reduce the need for children to work, or to improve the
quality and relevance of education so that school is perceived as a
worthwhile investment for poor children and families. These
measures may hold relatively few immediate lessons for UK policy
on children and work. Other important measures in the South are

---

* The term 'South' is preferred to 'developing countries' since it does not
imply catching up with the 'rich' countries of the North.

aimed at eliminating or reducing the hazardous and exploitative elements of their work. Enforcement of legislation, voluntary initiatives on the part of employers, and grassroots and trade union action to encourage employers to improve children's and adults' working conditions are among the main strategies employed to achieve these goals. Similar strategies have been, and continue to be, used in the UK.

Child labour has primarily been conceived in both North and South as a problem that can primarily be addressed by the 'top-down' implementation of policies, informed and designed by 'experts'. However, the evidence of continued, and in some parts of the world growing, involvement of children in hazardous and exploitative work suggests that these policies alone will not solve the problem. The reasons for the failure of policies and legislation to protect working children are too numerous and complex to be discussed here.[4] However, one important factor is that laws and policies are often not based on a thorough understanding of working children's lives and experiences, and the role of work within their lives. In many countries, including the UK, law governing the employment of children is antiquated, and bears little relation to the kinds of work children do, or the problems they face at work. Thus, working children, their families, employers and law enforcers often perceive laws and policies as irrelevant, or as unwelcome interference, and disregard them.

One means of ensuring that policy and action on child labour is based on the realities of working children's and young people's lives is to involve them in developing 'solutions'. This approach, while relatively uncommon, has arisen primarily in the South, and is also of growing importance in international child labour debates. In the UK, by contrast, despite increasing participation of children and young people in decision-making on issues such as leisure services or living arrangements in custody cases, their insights on work have been largely ignored. Nor has there been much support for measures to assist children and young people themselves to challenge poor working conditions. This may be in large part due to the long-standing denial in the UK that there are problematic aspects to children's work.[5]

Involving children and young people in developing solutions to work-related problems is relatively new, and conclusions about its effectiveness in improving their situation are necessarily tentative. This chapter seeks to draw out lessons from existing experiences and assess their relevance for action on children and work issues in the UK.

INTERNATIONAL EXPERIENCES

Initiatives to promote children's and young people's involvement in policy and action on work issues take various forms and operate at a range of levels. Some aim primarily to promote change in the immediate situation of child participants, while others are aimed at changing policy on children and work. Many organisations now try to enhance their impact by doing both.

PARTICIPATION IN IDENTIFYING USEFUL SUPPORT SERVICES

It is still rare, though becoming more common, that services for working children and young people are designed in conjunction with them. However, failure to do so can result in services that, while appreciated by the children and young people concerned, do not meet their most pressing needs. For example, provision of free meals for street working children is common in many Latin American countries. However, discussion with the children themselves reveals that protection from police harassment is often their most pressing concern.[6]

While this example may seem only tangentially relevant to the situation of working children and young people in the UK, the principle that working children are able to identify the immediate problems that face them is clearly pertinent. This is an important principle for initiatives intending to support young workers directly rather than primarily through legislative reform.

WORKING CHILDREN'S AND YOUTH ORGANISATIONS[7]

Working children's and youth organisations (WCYOs) have developed over the last 20 years in Latin America, India, West Africa and, more recently, in various countries in South-East Asia. WCYOs take many forms and include groups of children and young people who come together spontaneously on the street to protect themselves from extortion or harassment, organisations supporting working children and young people in a particular district, and, in Latin America, where such organisations have the longest history, large national networks of working children.

WCYOs vary considerably in their visions concerning children and work, though improving children's working conditions is a short-term concern for all. The kind of support they offer to their members also varies considerably depending on local and organisational priorities and on the organisations' relationship to adult organisations. Most are linked to a supporting non-governmental organisation (NGO). These NGOs generally provide a range of support services to working children, including: informal education and skills training; credit and savings facilities (for the children and sometimes their families); assistance in obtaining documentation (eg, birth certificates, work permits or registration with police); and, in some cases, advocacy with employers on behalf of children. In some cases, these support services are organised by the children and young people themselves.

Several WCYOs have grown out of a refusal of adult trade unions to admit young members, or to address the concerns of young workers. Reasons for this include: legal constraints on children's membership of unions; a lack of interest in young workers' problems; difficulties faced by trade unions in organising the sectors where children and young people are concentrated; or a stance that allowing children to join workers' organisations legitimises child labour, which is often viewed as a cause of adult unemployment.

Given the diversity of children and young people's work, it is unsurprising that their motivations for joining such organisations vary. For some children and young people, making use of the services and support provided by the WCYO and/or its support organisations may be the main motivation for participating; for some, the hope of improving their working situation may be paramount. Others, particularly those in solitary occupations such as domestic work, may value the contact with and emotional support of other young workers; for others, the opportunity to get their voices heard may be the most important aspect.

The following quotation illustrates what participation in a WCYO has meant to a 13-year-old domestic worker from Dakar, Senegal:

> *We are trying to get organised so that we can improve children's working conditions. Before the movement [WCYO] was set up, we had many difficulties with education, health care and not feeling that we had the right to be respected. We have many problems with our employers, especially in my work as a housemaid. Sometimes they don't pay us for two or three months. If we protest, sometimes they beat us. Also if you accidentally break something they want you to pay for it. If you are sick, there is no health insurance ... It was because of these types of problems that we decided to organise ... For example, we have set up our own health care fund. We have also arranged for*

schooling in the evening when we are not working ... There are certain things our employers wouldn't dare to do now.[18]

Similarly, for members of Bal Mazdoor Sangh (the Child Workers' Union) in Delhi, India, one of the most important aspects of organising has been that harassment by adult market traders is much reduced. These examples suggest that participation in WCYOs has been empowering for the children and young people concerned in that it has enhanced their control over aspects of their lives.

While working children and young people clearly value peer support and organising with other young people, trade unions, NGOs and other organisations can play a vital role in helping children and young people achieve better working conditions. Partnership between WCYOs and 'adult' organisations may be critical in getting issues of concern to children and young people taken seriously.

PARTICIPATION IN LOCAL REPRESENTATIVE STRUCTURES, POLICY AND PLANNING FORA

In the South, as in the UK, formal involvement of children and young people in local representative structures, policy fora or planning initiatives is not common. Where children and young people's views are sought locally, this generally takes place through one-off consultations, which at best inform local decision-making bodies, but which are rarely formally integrated into them. However, there are a few examples of local representative bodies developing more formal structures for listening to children and young people on issues that affect them, including work.

For example, in southern India an NGO, the Concerned for Working Children (CWC), has helped working children and young people to develop their own organisation – Bhima Sangha. In addition to assisting children to leave hazardous work and to obtain an education or skills training, CWC has supported Bhima Sangha groups to make their voices heard in village councils. This has led to the formation of village taskforces to address issues of concern to villagers, including children. One of the problems identified by Bhima Sangha members is the degradation of natural resources close to villages. This means that village families, including children, have to migrate seasonally in order to find work, and women and children have to walk long distances to collect fodder and fuel. Another common problem was the poor maintenance of village paths, meaning that in the wet season children could not reach school.

As a result, some community leaders have changed decisions about the use of natural resources under their jurisdiction, so land degradation has started to be reversed, or have ensured that paths to schools are properly maintained. Children who have participated in local councils state that in addition to the satisfaction of seeing their suggestions taken up locally, they have become more confident through speaking up to village authorities. This has been particularly important for girls, who usually have fewer opportunities to speak out in public.[9]

PARTICIPATION IN INTERNATIONAL POLICY-MAKING ON CHILD LABOUR

Child labour is high on the international policy agenda. The International Labour Organisation is developing a new Convention on the Extreme Forms of Child Labour, various governments are taking unilateral action to tighten their legislation and introduce other programmes to combat child labour, and UNICEF, NGOs, trade unions and, most recently, the World Bank are giving the issue much greater priority.

The involvement of children and young people in international meetings on child labour is a new phenomenon. In 1997, for the first time, working children and young people participated in international conferences in Amsterdam and Oslo, and in regional consultations in Bangkok and Brasilia.[10] Although the space for them to speak in the official meetings varied, they were able to promote their views and experiences through meetings with delegates, and to obtain considerable media coverage.

It is too early to assess the impact of children's and young people's participation in international debates. However, a few observations can be made. The substance of conference declarations and agendas for action appears to have changed little.[11] However, anecdotal evidence from the Oslo Child Labour Conference suggests that some delegates were influenced by the views of the children and young people present. Perhaps more importantly, the fact of their presence seems to be shifting the balance of opinion towards recognising them as important stakeholders, though there is still opposition to this. If this results in a greater readiness to include working children's perspectives in national plans of action, the impact may be far greater than that suggested solely by their presence in international meetings.

It is notable that despite an increasing number of initiatives at local and international level, little attention has so far been paid to involving children and young people in policy and action on work issues at national level. Given that legislation is developed and implemented at national level, developing such initiatives should be a priority.

LESSONS FROM INTERNATIONAL EXPERIENCE

This section summarises some of the broader lessons that can be drawn from international experience of involving children and young people in policy and action on work issues. Several of these apply more directly to policy-related consultations than to action to improve children's and young people's conditions in specific workplaces. However, some, such as ensuring that children and young people are able to express their views without intimidation, and that they have sufficient information to make decisions, apply anywhere. These issues may be readily apparent to readers who work in a participatory way with children, young people, or adults. I raise them here as background to the subsequent suggestions for enhancing children's and young people's involvement in policy and action on work issues in the UK.

CRITICAL IMPORTANCE OF ACCURATE INFORMATION

It is evident from international experience that children and young people can make significant contributions to local policy and action based on their own experience. For children and young people to be able to participate effectively in national and international debates, and for their views to be given credence by others, it is essential that as well as arguing from direct experience, they are well informed of wider issues. This implies an adequate preparation process for young participants in such consultations, so that they are not at risk of responding to inaccurate information and rumours.

BALANCING DIFFERENT VIEWS AND INTERESTS

Effective policy and action always involves balancing the views and interests of a number of stakeholders. While recognising the importance of children's and young peoples' direct experience, this needs to be set in the context of the views of other stakeholders who, through experience, may be able to see broader issues more clearly. Balancing these two potentially conflicting perspectives can be challenging at times.

IMPORTANCE OF GOOD FACILITATION

Ensuring that children and young people are able to express their views freely without intimidation or interference from adults, or from other children with different viewpoints, is critical. This points to the importance of good facilitation.

REPRESENTATIVENESS

In international debates, it is often charged that working children's and young people's representatives are not sufficiently representative of the diversity of child workers, especially those involved in the most hazardous and exploitative forms of work. Representing the diversity of children's occupations, while also striving for regional and gender balance, is clearly challenging, particularly where numbers of young delegates are strictly limited. Further, working children's and young people's organisations may follow their own democratic principles when selecting representatives, which may not accord with externally-derived criteria for overall balance in such fora. However, it is clear that to avoid young workers' opinions being dismissed purely on grounds of their (lack of) representativeness, it is desirable that a wide range of experiences are represented in conferences and consultations.

THE UK CONTEXT

PARTICIPATION IN WORK-ORIENTED ORGANISATIONS

It is evident that participation in a WCYO may have a range of benefits for young workers in the South. Might such organisations be helpful for working children and young people in the UK? Existing research with working children and young people suggests not in this form. The children and young people interviewed in Save the Children's research did not, on the whole, view clubs and/or networks for working children as a priority (see Chapter 4). The exception was children and young people working in isolation from their peers in rural Scotland, who felt that such networks would be useful.[12] The general lack of interest in organisations of this kind is not necessarily surprising. Work may play a relatively smaller role in the lives of children who work part time in the UK than it does for children working full time in the South. Many of the services that WCYOs provide to their members are already available to working and non-working children and young people in the UK. However, the interest shown in a complaints procedure to address grievances at work suggests there may be a need for at least one of the main functions of WCYOs – supporting members in advocacy with their employers and with authorities.

A review of existing structures in the UK suggests that trade unions might be the most appropriate body through which children and young people could address workplace problems. However, in the UK as in many other countries, although children aged 13 can legally work part time, very few trade unions are open to membership of young workers under 16, the minimum age for full-time employment. This means that one potentially valuable source of protection at work is denied to them. The failure of the current regulation system means that the majority of working children are unprotected.

Since 1989, one trade union – the GMB – has encouraged children and young people under 16 to become members, in one region waiving the membership fee for young workers. Anecdotal evidence suggests that union membership has enabled children to challenge abusive working practices.[13] Encouraging children and young people to join unions, perhaps in youth sections, and more active campaigning on the part of unions for adequate pay and protection for young workers could play an important role in improving their working conditions. It is heartening that the International Confederation of Free Trade Unions is encouraging its national affiliates to prioritise recruitment and protection of young workers as part of its drive to eliminate hazardous and exploitative child labour worldwide. Greater involvement of young people in existing unions might be more effective in the UK than forming separate 'young people's unions', which are liable to be ignored by employers. Advocating greater unionisation among young workers has, however, to be viewed in the context of a general decline in union membership in the UK over the last 20 years, an erosion of trade union rights and the fact that many of the sectors where children work are not unionised.

PARTICIPATION IN CONSULTATIONS AND LOCAL REPRESENTATIVE STRUCTURES

The scope for children and young people to put their views to local and national policy-makers in the UK has increased substantially over the last few years, but is still somewhat limited. A Save the Children review of children's and young people's participation in public decision-making in the UK concluded that

> although some local authorities are sympathetic, the prevailing political climate and absence of a unifying political framework means that the actions taken by individual authorities tend to be piecemeal, arbitrary and limited in scope ... The Children Act has been important in setting out the principle of consulting children, but the practice needs more commitment from institutions and individuals.[14]

At present, structures in which children and young people can express their opinions include: school councils, though by no means all schools have these; local Agenda 21 initiatives where children and young people can put their views on local environmental issues; and consultations organised by local authorities on services used by children and young people. There are also initiatives to elicit young people's views on a more structured basis. For example, Devon County Council has established a youth council that meets regularly; the Manchester Young People's Forum organises regular meetings for children and young people aged 12-15 to speak out on issues of concern to panels of decision-makers. These panels usually comprise local authority councillors, MPs and topic experts. So far, issues discussed have included health, racism, drug awareness and the environment.[15]

More initiatives of this kind could provide a forum for young people to voice their views and concerns on work issues throughout the country. By increasing officials' levels of awareness of the issues facing children and young people at work, they could play an important role in encouraging greater action by local authorities to enforce the law and protect children from unacceptable working conditions. The issues raised in such fora could also be fed into national debates on work issues, and could play an important role in informing national policy. As in the Indian example discussed earlier, such participation might also be rewarding personally for children and young people.

The current government review of legislation pertaining to children and employment in the UK presents an important opportunity to ensure that policy-makers are aware of working children's and young people's concerns. This need be no paper exercise – the research discussed in this book indicates that children and young people have plenty to say about work, legislation, and how their working lives could be improved. If local consultative structures cannot be set up on a more widespread basis and used to channel children's and young people's views to policy-makers, consultations should be organised regionally for this purpose. This should not, however, be a substitute for establishing more formal local consultative processes on work issues or using existing structures for such consultations.

CONCLUSIONS

This chapter looked at some international initiatives to increase children's and young people's involvement in policy and action on work issues. Although such initiatives are relatively few in number and recent, it appears that they have played an important role in ensuring that local action to improve children's and young people's working conditions takes their views and experiences into account. Working children and young people are also beginning to make their voices heard in international child labour debates. While it is important not to over-generalise from a small number of experiences, it appears that participation in such initiatives can lead to more effective action and policy, and may also contribute to children's and young people's development. It could therefore be an important aspect of developing new legislation and a more workable regulation system for children's and young people's work in the UK. Although structures for consulting with children and young people on work-related issues are limited, this paper has outlined several ways in which existing initiatives could be expanded. For example, local council consultations with children and young people could ensure that work issues are also covered; trade unions could ensure that they recruit working children and young people and represent their concerns.

Meaningful involvement of children and young people is not simply a matter of gathering a handful together and asking them to talk about work! It involves ensuring that young participants have access to adequate information to make informed decisions; it requires skilled facilitation to balance different views and interests and to ensure that some participants are not intimidated or marginalised. It may also require extensive preparation, and advocacy work with authorities who dispute the value of such processes.

Involving children and young people in discussions and action on work-related issues is clearly only one of a number of measures that could contribute to better protection for working children and young people in the UK (see Chapters 1, 4 and 9). Nor is direct involvement of children and young people the only way in which their views and experiences can influence policy – research that draws on children's and young people's experiences can also play a vital and complementary role. However, recognition of the complexities of involving children and young people in policy and action on work issues, and of other approaches to addressing children and work issues, should not obscure the contribution that their participation can make.

NOTES

1 For a detailed analysis of the reasons children work in the South today, see R Marcus and C Harper, *Small Hands: children in the working world*, Working Paper 16, Save the Children, 1996.

2 See V Morrow, 'Responsible children? Aspects of children's work and employment in contemporary UK', in B Mayall (ed), *Children's Childhoods Observed and Experienced*, Falmer Press, 1994; Middleton *et al* (this volume); Leonard (this volume) for insights into this issue.

3 See Morrow, *ibid*, and M Lavalette, S Hobbs, S Lindsay and J McKechnie, 'Child employment in Britain: policy, myth and reality', *Youth and Policy*, Winter 1994/95, on the UK; Lee-Wright, *The Child Slaves*, Earthscan, 1990, and N Burra, *Born to Work: child labour in India*, Delhi, Oxford University Press, 1995, for Asian examples.

4 See Marcus and Harper (note 1) for more detailed analysis.

5 M Lavalette *et al* (see note 3).

6   J Ennew, *Street and working children: a guide to planning*, Development Manual 4, Save the Children, 1994.

7   This section is based primarily on discussions with members of WCYOs and their support organisations at the Oslo International Conference on Child Labour in October 1997.

8   Cited in Save the Children, *Save the Children Communication Toolkit, Briefing on Child Labour*, December 1997, International Save the Children Alliance, Geneva, 1997.

9   This section is based on N Singh and R Trivedy, *Approaches to Child Participation: a discussion paper*, Save the Children, South and Central Asia Regional Office, Kathmandu, 1996, and on discussions with Bhima Sangha members and Concerned for Working Children staff at the Oslo International Conference on Child Labour in October 1997.

10 Despite pressure from WCYOs, they were not invited to, nor allowed to speak at, regional consultations in Lahore and Pretoria respectively.

11 It is, of course, common for such agendas to be substantially agreed in advance of international conferences.

12 Bridget Pettitt, personal communication.

13 Steve Pryle, GMB Union, personal communication.

14 SCF, *All together now. Community participation for children and young people*, Save the Children, 1997, p27.

15 *Ibid*, p31.

9 Child employment legislation: changing the focus

Ben Whitney

What are child employment rules for? There has been no serious discussion in this country about what we are trying to achieve since the current framework was formulated in the 1930s. Is the basis of the regulations a concern for children's welfare and safety, the protection of the working rights of adults, or a fear that work may interfere with formal education and 'family life'? The focus is unclear. Every 'review' leaves things almost entirely unchanged and as uncertain as before.

This chapter looks at the current legislative framework and at the expectations on local education authorities regarding its enforcement. Without a change in emphasis which recognises the fact that children work and always have done, the current system can provide no more than an illusion of effective regulation. There has to be a complete re-think of the relationship between 'work' and 'education' and, at the end of the chapter, is a series of recommendations for improvement.

THE LEGAL FRAMEWORK

The law is concerned only with children of compulsory school age, (ie, up to the *end* of their final year of compulsory education), who 'assist in a trade or occupation carried on for profit', not with all children who work. Washing your dad's car is not employment; going with him to the garage where he works and washing the cars on the forecourt is, even if the child isn't paid for either task! Children working in their parent's business are covered, but children working for themselves are not as there is no employer. There are additional regulations covering children who take part in 'performances' (theatre, TV, film, etc), and some controls over 'modelling' and other kinds of entertainments, though there are many exemptions.

The rules are a mixture of national legislation, (primarily the Children and Young Persons Act 1933 and the Employment of Women, Young Persons and Children Act 1920) and local authority byelaws. There is some variation, but in general:

- children may not work at all before the age of 13 (with certain exceptions);
- they may work no more than two hours on a school day, with a maximum of one hour before school;
- they may not work before 7am or after 7pm on *any* day, including school holidays;
- on Saturdays and school holidays a child may work up to five hours a day (aged 13/14) or eight hours (aged 15/16) subject to weekly maximums;
- Sunday working is restricted to two hours between 7am and 7pm.

Some workplaces are entirely prohibited for children, including all 'industrial undertakings' – a very wide definition of any kind of work which involves making or preparing articles for sale, and 'commercial kitchens' such as chip shops and burger bars. Children cannot serve alcohol or sell Lottery tickets and local authorities may have a variety of other prohibitions. It is likely that a more standard list of prohibited employments will emerge from the Department of Health in 1998, with a wide range of restrictions. Children of 13 will be permitted to do only work on a prescribed list. The somewhat belated implementation of the EC Directive on children at work (94/33/EC) should at least lead to greater consistency, but it is already largely in line with UK legislation and local education authorities are free to make amendments.

HOW THE CURRENT FRAMEWORK IS ENFORCED

Local education authorities (LEAs) have been responsible for the regulation of children in the workplace since the imposition of universal secondary education in the late nineteenth century. An employer should apply for a licence or permit in each child's case and, provided the employment is within the regulations, the LEA gives the necessary approval. Medical checks can be required and the LEA has the power to remove approval where the employment may be affecting the child's health, welfare or education.[1] It is an offence to employ a child, even a member of your own family, without this permission.

LEAs have limped along for years with varying degrees of commitment to what is frequently only a paper exercise, while most children have worked, but outside the boundaries of what they are supposed to do, or in work not subject to any regulation.[2] Few LEAs would claim that they do much more than scratch the surface of those who should be licensed. Most newsagents are aware of the regulations and local licensing systems are dominated by newspaper deliverers. But many who employ children only occasionally or who employ their own children never come to the LEA's attention.

Regulation has traditionally been a low priority for LEAs – frequently under-resourced to a point where the system can only react to information when it is received. Some smaller metropolitan authorities have been more proactive. There are very few prosecutions (no national statistics are available). The system has been largely successful in ensuring that children do not go out to work when they should be at school, though there are sometimes difficulties over 16-year-olds leaving school and getting a job early. We have at least advanced this far since the nineteenth century. But this is hardly an adequate measure of overall effectiveness when illegal working is so widespread.

AN OUTDATED FRAMEWORK

Any objective assessment must accept that the current framework does not reflect the realities of the twenty-first century. It is simply out-dated. The intention of the original legislation was to cover children between the ages of 13 and the then school leaving age of 14. It now includes those who are nearly 17. Virtually every other aspect of children's lives has been radically affected by changing societal expectations since the 1930s – from the 'discovery' of child abuse and two extensions of the school leaving age to the creation of a teenage culture. The concept of 'Gillick competency', following a 1985 court ruling that a child under 16 may seek health care and advice without the consent of their parent, has, together with the Children Act 1989, enabled children to make a far greater range of decisions for themselves. It is incredible that their rights and role in the workplace are assumed to have remained more or less the same throughout this period. A whole variety of new employment opportunities have arisen along with all the other changes.

Once you are 16 you can leave home, legally have heterosexual sex, marry, play the Lottery and purchase tobacco products. It now seems odd that your working life must still be restricted to two hours after school or to no later than 7pm in the middle of a school holiday! For many families, it is only when the young person wants to leave school before they are able, that they discover that the part-time work which they are already doing is also illegal, though it may have continued without incident for some time. Virtually everyone – employers, parents, teachers and children themselves – claims not to have been aware of the regulations before.

PUBLIC AMBIVALENCE

LEAs are also faced with a widespread ambivalence about their regulatory role. Despite concerns about safety and exploitation, society is unclear about what view it should take about children and work; this inevitably affects those who are expected to control it. As shown in earlier chapters of this book, children have always worked, they like to do it and, in general, it is often seen as a positive and affirming part of their personal development. Children showing enterprise and initiative are commended by politicians, parents and the media. Work is not always seen as exploitative and inappropriate. Yet much of what children actually do outside school is illegal and local education authorities are regularly castigated for failing to stop it.

It is wholly unrealistic to suggest that courts be used more frequently simply for infringements of byelaws and rules such as working over two hours on a Sunday or after 7pm on a Saturday. (This is about as likely as someone being prosecuted for letting their dog foul the pavement!) The collection of evidence is time-consuming and complicated, requiring out-of-hours working which is not likely to be adequately resourced. There are also questions of justice and reasonableness to be faced when the infringements are so common. Even if court action is taken, the offence is trivial and the penalty only minor unless there are also much more serious questions of health and safety (prosecutions which are not undertaken by the LEA itself).

There are endless anomalies and weaknesses within the existing system which make enforcement difficult. Few people realise that their offer of a part-time job, even to their own children, should be licensed. Consequently, there are thousands of children working illegally on farms, in corner shops, etc, where the parent and the employer are the same person. Where does 'work' (for example, looking after horses, which apparently involves 400,000 children) become 'employment'? Why should the hours children spend delivering newspapers be so tightly regulated when they can spend far greater hours each week, often early in the morning or late at night, in sports training, competitions and other activities? These too can be the context for abuse and exploitation. Why should what children do on Sundays and in school holidays be regulated by those responsible for their education? What logic dictates that 7.30 in the evening, even in the middle of August, is an unsuitable time for a child to be working, or, indeed, that 7am on a dark and rainy February morning *is* suitable?

THE BENEFITS TO CHILDREN

Most importantly of all, what does the current framework actually offer to children themselves? What practical difference does it make to a child whether or not they have been licensed by their employer? It offers them no real protection, nor any guarantee of good practice. It may safeguard their welfare to some extent with a responsible employer and deter some of those who are totally unsuitable. But there is widespread anecdotal evidence that if children protest at being asked to work outside the regulations, even when they are legally licensed, they are likely to be dismissed, and there is little or nothing the LEA can do to prevent it. They simply have to license their replacement!

The much-quoted suggestion that a child will not be covered by the employer's insurance if they are not licensed appears not to be universally true; many insurance companies do not check when a claim is made for a bicycle stolen during a paper round, etc. Employers have a general liability to everyone on their premises, not only to their employees. Whether or not the work was legally registered is often not an issue. Neither does the current system in any way regulate the payment of adequate wages or the practice of 'fining' child employees who arrive late or who fail to meet some other requirement imposed by the employer over which the LEA has no control. An employer may keep scrupulously to the rules but still be wholly unreasonable in their treatment of their employees.

Crucially, the licensing system gives the LEA no power to check on the *character* of the employer and whether or not s/he is a suitable person to employ children. It attempts to prevent children from doing dangerous activities, though some of these concepts are now hopelessly out of date, but the regulations contain no provision at all regarding dangerous *individuals*. The man running the corner shop may be a Schedule 1 Offender under the Children and Young Persons Act 1933, with a history of criminal convictions for abuse against children, but the LEA has no power to check his background and must issue licences for such work provided the hours are legal. This offers a child no 'protection' at all worth speaking of.

SAFETY

Clearly children's work should be safe, but it is not always easy to see why their employment is so tightly regulated compared with other aspects of their lives. Figures from the Child Accident Prevention Trust (CAPT), compiled from official statistics, show that there are many other situations in which children may be injured or even killed. In 1995, 730,000 children aged 10-15 were hurt in sports accidents; over 133,000 children under 15 were injured in the garden, almost a million were injured at home. While research into children at work has shown that many children do have accidents,[3] there is little basis for being able to make any meaningful national comparison with figures like these.

Research by the CAPT found that accidents at work were under-reported but that few official statistics are available.[4] Undoubtedly work does lead to injuries (though not all are related to 'employment') but no one knows exactly where work fits in the scale of all the risks faced by children. If safety were the primary concern, paper rounds would probably be the first casualty. Where employers have failed to carry out the necessary 'risk assessment', enforcement is the responsibility of either the Health and Safety Executive or local authority Environmental Health Officers, not the LEA. The LEA's role is restricted only to hours, etc, which means that legal workplaces which are nonetheless unsafe may not be easily identified, especially where interdepartmental co-ordination is poor.

REGULATING 'PERFORMANCES'

The system for regulating entertainments, under separate legislation, is equally shot through with difficulties. The LEA should issue a licence for each child who takes part in commercial performances/ entertainments. The law seems primarily designed for those few children who have the opportunity to pursue a professional career, but it leaves unregulated many activities which might still be exploitative in terms of the time demanded or the lack of financial reward for the children's services.

Definitions are unclear, though the scope of the regulations is being extended. There was considerable debate amongst education welfare professionals when two girls aged 13 and 14 took part in a boxing match. This might well have been appropriately classed as an illegal 'dangerous performance' because it was taking place in a night club before a paying audience, though this was not universally agreed. Had it been in a more conventional amateur sporting context, no question as to its legality would have been raised any more than it is for boys. Similarly, children are allowed to use shotguns at a clay pigeon range, and even to work there if it is a 'private club' rather than a commercial business. Children drive mini stock cars, ride scramble bikes and take all kinds of risks in settings not covered by the performance licence system.

There are enormous uncertainties surrounding 'modelling' which may, or may not, be seen by an LEA as requiring licensing, though the Department of Health has been attempting to clarify this area. Many of the regulations seem to imply a risk about the worlds of film, theatre and television which is quaint and rather patronising, using terms such as 'matrons' and 'moral welfare'. These regulations too have failed to keep up with changes in culture. They allow a privileged few to use their talents for considerable financial reward in a way which is denied to most other children, when their peers who are spending endless hours in semi-professional football coaching are overlooked. Children lucky enough to be in film, TV and the theatre *can* have time off school, and considerable amounts of it, unlike any other working children.

CURRENT AND FUTURE TRENDS

In truth, the current system for both employment and performances makes little difference to anyone and has been largely ignored for generations. Attempts to implement it more thoroughly result only in frustration for everyone involved. It looks to children, parents and employers as if local bureaucracy is simply trying to stifle initiative and opportunity. Children want to work. Even allowing for the need to sometimes stop them doing what they would like to do because it is not appropriate, the system is irksome and generally unhelpful in trying to build a modern relationship between young people and the world of formal employment.

From 1998 the UK will have met the requirements of the 1994 EC Directive, though this has resulted in little or no change to the existing system, beyond the introduction of a 'compulsory' two-week break from work in the school holidays which would be hugely unpopular with children if enforced. There are signs that the current Labour government is taking a generally more restrictive line than its predecessor, though an even more interventionist Private Member's Bill did not receive official backing. The Directive limits the number of hours a child may work to below previous levels and the Government may choose not to make use of the opt-outs which allowed longer working hours here. There appears to be a general climate in the Department of Health and Department for Education and Employment that children should be concentrating on their homework and family life; Sundays are not now considered a suitable day for children to be employed as was previously proposed.

Yet again, the nettle is not being grasped and LEAs will be expected to continue enforcing regulations which everyone knows are being widely ignored and which are generally unenforceable. Such a situation should not be sustained any longer; unless there are changes, the whole question of regulating child employment will simply remain an irrelevant anachronism. LEAs will not be prepared to resource work which appears to make no effective contribution to ensuring children's welfare and which does not enjoy general public support. There is a wide range of issues to be addressed if the job is to be done properly.

A NATIONAL DEBATE

First of all, there has to be a serious national debate about the place of children in the workforce and what they should and should not do. This has to be more than either the general denial that there is a problem or further exhortations on LEAs to try harder. There needs to be a proper and informed discussion, based on recent research, not a constant re-telling of what we already know without any recognition of the implications.

It is no good, for example, simply wishing that children would spend more time on homework without recognising the economic reality that many children, and most of their parents, will always choose activities which bring some financial reward, given the opportunity. Through work, children have the chance to contribute something to their family life and to achieve a degree of independence. Such behaviour is surely to be commended, provided there are no wider questions of health, safety or educational disadvantage which are being ignored in the quest for cash.

Some attempt should be made to quantify the contribution that children make to the economy. Employers, teachers, parents and politicians should make opportunities to listen to children and to take account of *their* views on what they should and should not do. It was noticeable in the consultation process to gather responses to the EC Directive carried out by the previous government that the views of children themselves were neither sought nor heard. This is in marked contrast to the contribution which children are making directly to the debate about child labour in an international context (see Chapter 8). There must be a change of climate which recognises what is going on and asks key questions about what kind of system is now appropriate for a new millennium.

There also needs to be greater guidance given on work which does not require an approved employer, such as babysitting, etc. This actually accounts for the bulk of what children do. Some young people are effectively working for themselves (as gardeners, car-cleaners, etc), or working for people who are not commercial employers. It is unfortunate that many of the surveys include these kinds of activities without making it clear that they are entirely outside the regulations. This tends to give the impression that LEAs are even more remiss than is in fact the case. Probably no more than half the 'work' done by children is appropriately classed as 'employment' and could not effectively be regulated by any agency, only by parents using their common sense. This should be clearly recognised.

A MORE MEANINGFUL PROCEDURE

Something must be done to make the regulation and licensing procedure more meaningful. There will be no greater commitment to it, by employers, parents, children or local authorities, while its purpose is so unclear. As well as the need to update the regulations so as to allow, especially older, children much more opportunity and flexibility than currently exist, the whole emphasis needs to shift away from the individual child and onto the *employer*. I am not convinced that LEAs need to know the details of each child's individual working hours right down to the last paper girl/boy. Far more important is the fact that the person for whom they are working, and the work which they are doing, is suitable and safe. The key regulators of what is suitable for children should be their parents; some licensing systems have not even required their consent. Only a tiny minority would act irresponsibly if given greater status and information within the procedures.

A much better system would be to require employers to register with the LEA (or perhaps with some other department of the local authority such as Social Services or Environmental Health), and to operate under a *nationally-agreed* Code of Practice. It would still be an offence by parents under attendance law to allow their children to work when they should be at school; children whose attendance is unsatisfactory should still be covered by other procedures. Employers would have to agree to a police check, provide character references and undertake to operate according to agreed standards. The individual contract of employment should be between the employer, the child and the parent, with perhaps a requirement only to send to the local authority a list of names, addresses, etc, every six months.

Local authorities should concentrate their attention on regulating the employer, not the children; dealing with any complaints; enforcing standards; and, crucially, have the power to withdraw approved status from any employer found to be unsuitable. It would be an offence to employ children without first obtaining such approved status or following its removal. This would be a much more manageable workload and give the local authority real 'teeth', without being expected to use the courts in response to even minor examples of poor practice. Withdrawing approved status from a newsagent would effectively put that shop out of business. This would be work of real value, not merely a paper-chase which makes no difference. Courts need only be used *in extremis*, especially where there are wider offences as well.

PROPOSAL FOR A NEW CODE OF PRACTICE

What would such a Code of Practice look like? What would be the appropriate expectations for a modern approach to the employment of children? Granted that the EC Directive may impose certain limitations, there is room for considerable change to the existing rules.

There must be a clear definition of what is covered by this procedure and what is not.
We can never hope to regulate all 'work', only 'employment'. The problem with the definition of 'a trade or occupation carried on for profit' is that it appears to leave out a number of potential employers: charities, public authorities, schools, private clubs, etc. There are countless children working for 'non-profit-making' employers whose employment is unregulated as a result. A new framework should contain a much clearer list of commercial settings as the area which the law wishes to regulate; there would then need to be further definitions of what kinds of work are prohibited altogether and what is outside the scope of the regulations. This is not an easy process, but the existing definition is not sufficient. This is also important in relation to entertainments where there needs to be much greater clarity about which activities the local authority is supposed to be regulating. There is wide variation here simply because we do not know what is covered by the term 'performance'.

Children working in their own parents' business should be exempt, provided that the work is not on the list of prohibited employments and is not done in school time.
'Factories' (or some other word less all-embracing than 'industrial undertaking') and other environments considered unsuitable for children would still need to be prohibited. Pubs, as such, might not need to be prohibited entirely, though clearly the serving of alcohol

should be. Parents using work experience as part of their 'education otherwise' programme would still require some regulation and monitoring to ensure that the child was not simply working in place of any formal education.

A daily and weekly maximum number of hours should be set, and it would have to be the child's parent who would be legally responsible for ensuring this, as an individual employer might not be aware that the child is working elsewhere as well.

The contract between the employer, parent and child would need to contain a declaration that the child was not working beyond the permitted limits. Personally, I can see no reason why the permitted hours cannot be more generous in school holidays than in term time, with higher limits for older children. The 7pm deadline could be replaced immediately by 8pm for 15/16-year-olds without infringing the EC Directive. (I would not change 7am as the earliest a child may work, even though it is widely ignored.) There should certainly be greater flexibility at weekends, with a whole weekend limit which treats Sundays in the same way as Saturdays. There is no reason why a child should not work one day or the other; prohibiting Sunday working *per se* takes no account of de-regulation or the fact that Sunday has no religious significance for millions of families, including those from minority cultures. All of this would enable many responsible employers to employ children on a legal basis where they cannot currently do so.

The employer would be responsible for obtaining the necessary approval to employ children, including checks on their personal character and suitability, and for notifying the local authority of children in their employment.

This does not need to be approval for each individual child, especially as many children only work for a very short time, provided that all children employed are over the necessary minimum age and are not exceeding their total weekly and daily hours. Employers would also be required to operate within an agreed guide to employment rights, which could not have the force of law, but which would give children and parents the right to complain if the employer failed to protect their health and welfare or acted unreasonably and could even define a minimum wage. If children are responsible enough to work, they are entitled to the same kind of protection as is afforded to other workers. Persistent failings could result in withdrawal of approval, for which there would have to be some kind of appeals procedure. There would obviously have to be a widespread public information campaign to ensure that employers, parents and children were aware of the new approach. This cannot be left to individual local authorities acting in isolation.

LINKS TO WORK EXPERIENCE

It is odd that while acknowledging that 'work experience' is a vital part of children's education, we are not giving due regard to their 'experience of work', which may have gone on for years, not just for a couple of weeks. The National Record of Achievement which pupils compile during their final year of compulsory education asks them to include details of their part-time work, but no information is requested or offered about what is and is not legal.

Official (unpaid) work experience can now take place at any time in secondary school years 10 and 11. Some children are being given much greater opportunity than others, especially those disaffected with the conventional curriculum. It is extremely confusing for children, parents and employers if the LEA/school is one moment encouraging them to have more work-based experience and the next seeking to prohibit what they are doing outside school and in their holidays. There is a danger that teachers will view part-time employment entirely negatively, as being always in competition with education. It may be, however, that the discipline of the workplace is essential in preventing the child from becoming entirely disaffected from all responsible activity. Education welfare officers are often faced with a dilemma around whether adhering to the letter of the law is more important than recognising what motivates a particular young person and building upon it.

It is possible for a teenager to go right through secondary school and never formally address the issue of their part-time employment – with no discussion on its legality, safety, financial fairness or, for that matter, its possible impact on their education. 'Better to pretend they're not working' or 'we don't want to be seen to be encouraging it' seem to be common sentiments in schools. The issues need to be tackled much more openly. Schools could ensure that learning opportunities are created out of the work which children do, so that the two can be seen as complementary rather than in competition.

At the other extreme, schools have sometimes encouraged children to work, with a complete lack of awareness of the regulations. A high school in my authority hit upon the idea of 'marketing' their pupils to the local business community. They wrote to dozens of local employers, many of whom would be illegal workplaces for children, inviting them to advertise vacancies in the school! This was all described as 'work experience', even though the work was to take place outside school hours and for payment; no clear distinction was made between sixth formers and younger pupils and no mention was made of the fact that much of the employment would first have to be licensed by the LEA.

Equally, work experience co-ordinators in schools may encourage pupils to continue with successful placements at weekends and school holidays; even careers officers are not always aware of the rules and may assist children to obtain illegal employment. This is all evidence that employment may actually be seen as a positive experience, but without a proper and open awareness of the boundaries within which it should operate and a proper place in the educational curriculum. There is clearly a need for a more coherent and consistent approach if LEAs are to have any hope of effective regulation.

CONCLUSION

A changed approach would free education authority staff to concentrate on the 'bigger picture' rather than requiring every child who delivers newspapers to be individually licensed according to what are increasingly seen as rather petty rules and regulations. There would be risks: of parents who failed to take their responsibilities seriously and unscrupulous employers who managed to keep the authorities at arm's length. Few could deny, however, that such possibilities exist now and that the heavy concentration on individual licensing already makes it unlikely that resources will be available to do anything other than maintain a symbolic presence.

For the vast majority of children who work, no significant health, safety or educational issues appear to be raised, though the collection of more detailed statistics would clearly be helpful. Virtually all 'light work' outside school hours could become acceptable, given a more open climate in which employers are encouraged to see the value of reasonable rules which set out a generally agreed framework. Only a few would seek to flout them to excess. Parents colluding in their children avoiding school by working would continue to be covered by attendance legislation. With greater awareness in the community as a whole, they would be more easily identified as behaving unacceptably. Changing the focus of the whole framework would surely command more respect, not only from children, parents and employers, but also from those expected to enforce it.

NOTES

1   Section 559, Education Act 1996 – though only in relation to children who are registered pupils at a school, not, for example, those who are permanently excluded or educated 'otherwise'.

2   See, for example, Labour Research Group, *School children at work: A survey of local councils on the implementation of bye-laws on child employment*, GMB Union, 1995.

3   See, for example, C Pond and A Searle, *The Hidden Army: children at work in the 1990s*, Birmingham LEA/Low Pay Unit, 1991, and Chapter 6, this volume.

4   E Heptinstall, *Young Workers and their Accidents*, Child Accident Prevention Trust, 1997.

Conclusion: the way forward

Bridget Pettitt

Throughout this book, different chapters have looked at the various issues around children working and provided answers to some of the questions posed in the introduction. This conclusion draws together the broad themes that have emerged and makes recommendations on the basis of this evidence.

SUMMARY OF GENERAL THEMES

CHILDREN'S PARTICIPATION

A key theme running through this book is the importance of children and young people's involvement in the debate. The importance of involving children in decision-making has been demonstrated in the overseas context by Rachel Marcus (Chapter 8). Examples of programmes aimed at helping working children have shown that when children are consulted and are part of the planning process, these programmes are more appropriate to their needs. Working children's organisations and children participating in international debates have shown the importance of including children's perspectives, but children's voices have been lacking in the debate in this country. Only when the reality of children's lives is incorporated will recommendations be realistic and make a genuine difference to children. In Chapter 4, Save the Children attempts to address this. The chapter clearly portrays what children think about work and their own situation. It shows the strength of their desire to work, their motivation for working and the issues that they deal with as they work.

The need to get close to the issues that children face when working is reinforced by the diversity of contexts in which children are employed. Sue Middleton *et al*, Madeleine Leonard and Ben Whitney (Chapters 3, 5 and 9) all point out that any measures to assist children have to take into account their particular situation.

EXTENT AND NATURE OF CHILDREN'S WORK

As Michael Lavalette describes in Chapter 2, children in the UK have always worked and, although the context and nature of the work has changed, they still do in the 1990s. Research suggests that the majority of children have had experience of paid work before they reach the minimum school leaving age (16 years); Hobbs and McKechnie (Chapter 1) estimate that 1.4 million 11–15-year-olds work. Although the majority of working children are between 13 and 16 years of age, a small, but significant proportion of 11 and 12-year-olds work. The kind of work that children do is dominated by deliveries, babysitting, shop work and catering, although this masks the variety of jobs that children are employed in, for example, door-to-door selling, packing, gardening. The majority of children work for less than 10 hours a week (half working up to five hours). Less than a quarter work over 10 hours per week. Average earnings range from £1.60 to £2.34 an hour or £11.85 to £13.80 a week. Again this disguises wide variations, a small minority earning very low amounts of 50p or less an hour.

IS WORK A GOOD THING FOR CHILDREN?

This is the crucial question running through almost every chapter in this book. In Chapter 6, Ellen Heptinstall looks at the evidence of whether work is harmful or healthy for children. Certain aspects of work may be physically more harmful for children and young people than for adults – for example, lifting heavy weights, extremes of temperature and exposure to chemicals. Children also tire more easily. Evidence from the United States suggests that the types of jobs young people take on (which tend to be boring, repetitive and low paid) may not encourage a sense of responsibility or commitment and may make young people cynical about the world of work.

Work may be stressful and tiring, on top of the other commitments children have at home and at school. Although there is little conclusive evidence about the impact of work on children's education, it seems that those who work excessive hours do less well academically than those who work fewer hours.

In addition to this, there is strong evidence to show that children and young people are particularly susceptible to accidents at work. Some studies have shown that up to a third of children have had accidents while being employed. The majority of these accidents go unreported. Children are more at risk of accidents than adults owing to their inexperience and lack of understanding about risk, their attitudes to risk-taking and the type of jobs they take. Ben Whitney, however, argues in Chapter 9 that accidents to children at work need to be seen in the context of other risks children are exposed to – for example, in the home or playing sport. Research with children, both by Save the Children (SCF) and the Child Accident Prevention Trust (Chapters 4 and 6) found that the majority of children did not feel the work they did was dangerous, although they did prioritise the need for training and implementation of legislation on health and safety issues.[1]

The more positive aspects of work have been highlighted in many of the chapters. The research by SCF (Chapter 4) indicates that the majority of children interviewed felt that they were gaining from the work they did and their experience was a positive one. Children gain increased financial independence from their parents; this independence plays an important role in allowing children and young people to socialise with their friends. Earning money gives them a sense of self-esteem, they are often given responsibilities and treated in the main with respect. Many of the children found the work they did relieved boredom. There are also significant educational aspects to work, such as the way in which it develops the ability to work as part of a team, facilitating the transition from school to full-time work, and to relate to adults outside school and home.

The fundamental issue is the type of experience children are getting in their work. The range of jobs that children do and the context in which they are working is crucial to this analysis. This kind of evidence is often missed by large scale quantitative research and is better explored by qualitative in-depth studies. A wide range of experiences of work is reflected in the chapters of this book. For example, the children interviewed in SCF's research were working in a wide variety of jobs, in different circumstances. Positive and negative experiences are shown, and many of the differences may be related to the types of work being done. There may also be significant links between children's experience of work and the area in which they live, and the context in which they are working. For example, the Irish Traveller children (boys, in particular) saw their work as important to their future working lives.

However, despite their different circumstances and different experiences, children's attitudes towards their work were remarkably similar. It is therefore important to look at the differences between work contexts, but also to listen to children themselves for their perspectives on the work. What may seem to an adult a monotonous dead end job may be challenging and educational to a 13-year-old (see Chapter 7).

In order to determine whether work is beneficial or harmful to children there needs to be more analysis of the detail of the jobs they are doing. For example, 'shop work' could range from sweeping floors to stacking shelves, talking to customers or working on a till. Each of these different aspects of a job may have different levels of responsibility and make different demands on the child. Looking at work experience schemes in schools and children's career paths may be important to this analysis (see Chapter 7). By identifying what positive 'educational' benefits can come from work, each job that a child performs may be evaluated.

WHY DO CHILDREN WORK?

The phenomenon of children working in the past has been explained by a complex interaction of different influences and has been keenly debated. Lavalette gives a very detailed account of different arguments and economic influences in the past. It is no less complex now, and exploring this issue involves looking at different sources of information and the different contexts in which children work. Again, the first point is to listen to the reasons children themselves give for working: what motivates them to work; what are the perceived costs and benefits of work; and how they themselves weigh them up. It is also important to support this with an analysis of the context in which they are living. There are cultural expectations of children and their role, which may differ according to age, sex, ethnicity and class. The increased pressure for material goods in modern society and the concept of work as a virtue influences children's motivation to work. Broader socio-economic forces also have an effect. For example, the flexibility of the labour market and local employment patterns will define the type of work that is available to children and young people. The state of the economy will influence the level of demand for children's employment. Crucial to the analysis of children working is also an analysis of poverty.

LINKS TO POVERTY AND THE ECONOMY

In the past in the UK it was clearly the most disadvantaged children who worked (see Chapter 2). In developing countries, the primary reason for children working is still generally poverty (see Chapter 8). Unfortunately there has been very little research to explore the relationship between poverty and children working in the UK in the 1990s. Several chapters in this book begin to address this. It would appear from the limited evidence available that the propensity for a child to work is not directly linked with poverty, since children from more affluent homes are more likely to work than children in poorer families. The picture is not this simple, however. It may be that children from more affluent families live in areas with more ready access to jobs, or with parents with more potential contacts. There is some evidence to suggest that those children who live in low income families who do work are more likely to work longer hours than children from more affluent backgrounds.[3] This has important implications for these children's futures due to the close link between educational performance and longer hours of work.

Children from low income families were also paid at a lower rate. In Sue Middleton's study (Chapter 3), children living in families in receipt of income support were earning less than those living in families not on income support. In spite of working for a lower rate of pay, children in one parent families and in families on income support actually earn more per week than those in two parent families or those not on income support, due to the longer hours they work.

Middleton *et al* also find that working children make a significant contribution to household income. Children's earnings make up 2 per cent of the total net weekly income of their families, which increases to 6 per cent for families on income support or lone parents. Although this is not a high percentage in itself, the actual amount earned (£13 a week) would make a substantial difference to a low income family. Children also contributed indirectly to household income by spending their own earnings on things their parents would otherwise have had to pay for.

This evidence is also supported by findings in Chapters 4 and 5. In both studies, several of the children who work said that they gave money to their parents as they were particularly in need, thereby contributing directly to household income. Others also described buying essential items for themselves such as equipment and clothes for school. Children's contributions to the family are underestimated by looking at paid employment alone, particularly girls'. Children often make a substantial input in terms of domestic work and, as Madeleine Leonard finds in her study (Chapter 5), children's contribution to the household economy in terms of time (for example, working in the family business) can also be significant.[4]

GENDER

Although none of the chapters specifically focus on gender, the differences between girls' and boys' employment have arisen through-out the book (see, for example, Chapter 5). Girls are slightly less likely to have paid work than boys but the gap lessens as they get older. More significant is the different types of work that boys and girls do, which reflects the gender specific work patterns in the adult labour market. Girls are more likely to work in traditional 'female occupations' such as babysitting, waitressing and shop work. More boys do paper deliveries. Middleton *et al* also found that boys were more likely to have formal paid jobs than informal jobs. In their study, boys got better hourly rates than girls (£2.42 and £1.98 respectively).

A further interesting finding in terms of gender was the way work fits into children's lives. In the SCF study (Chapter 4), many girls said they would be doing unpaid domestic work if they did not have a paid job. The evidence suggests that children's early experiences of work are being structured by gender stereotypes which have strong implications for their future participation in work. In the SCF study, one girl said she had been sexually harassed at work.

LEGAL FRAMEWORK

The key way that the state aims to protect children from exploitation and harmful work in this country is through legislation.[5] As is discussed in the preceding chapters of this book, the legal framework around work is complicated and, it is argued, ineffectual. The majority of children who work are doing so illegally. A minority have a licence; many who work are under age, working in prohibited types of jobs or working outside the time restrictions. The views of the children in Chapter 4 show that many of the restrictions, especially those related to the hours they are allowed to work, make little sense to them. In Chapter 9, Ben Whitney, a local authority officer responsible for implementing the law, provides a critique of the legislation and makes proposals for change. The confusion outlined by Lavelette in Chapter 2 means that there is no coherent aim behind the current legislative framework, other than to ensure that children attend compulsory education. This, compounded by the fact that the law has not been realistically updated, means that it has become little more than a paper exercise.

RECOMMENDATIONS

1. A broader debate, based on sound evidence, is needed to establish what is acceptable work for children, and at what age. It must engage with all players: schools, education authorities, children and young people, parents, trade unions, and employers. Children and young people should be central contributors to the debate.
A balance needs to be established between protecting children and young people from exploitation and harmful and dangerous employment, and children's rights to participate in society, and to be recognised, both for their social contributions, directly through work itself, and indirectly through their views about work.

2. Children's voices must be listened to and mechanisms established for including children more effectively in decisions about their work – for example, via school councils, youth councils and junior membership of trade unions.

3. Legislation must be brought up to date to reflect the current realities of children's lives and must be designed to regulate children's work effectively.

A review of the legislation should look at the types of employment children are allowed to do and the times of day and week that they can work. It should look at effective methods of implementing the legislation. Several suggestions have been put forward for more effective methods of legislating for children's work. These include licensing the employer rather than each individual child and establishing a national code of conduct for children's employers, which would include police checking the employer (see Chapter 9).

4. More information is needed for both children and parents about their rights in the workplace.

Children can only make rational decisions about work and their safety by being given full information. Parents are key to supporting children in their work, regulating their hours and checking their safety (see Chapters 4, 6 and 9). Local authorities have the responsibility to produce information in a format that is accessible.

5. School and children's work should be linked more closely.

An education perspective can be very useful in establishing what elements of work are beneficial to children and young people at different ages. Schools can also usefully take on board the skills that children have learned from their part-time work and find ways of acknowledging this in the school students' records, and integrating aspects of students' part-time work into the curriculum. Schools are also effective routes for information flows to children and their parents, and should be encouraged to raise these issues. They should not be seen only in the context of 'policing' children's work.

6. Further research needs

While this book has endeavoured to collate a comprehensive range of research and information on children working in the UK, the gaps in the research and our knowledge of children working have been highlighted. Priority issues for new research are:

- **the connections between poverty and children's work.** The evidence indicates that it is poorer children who work the longest hours, are at most danger of being exploited, and whose education is most likely to suffer. Sufficient arguments have been made to demonstrate that issues of poverty and social exclusion need to be taken into account in all policies concerning children's employment. Policies aimed at preventing, or broadening, the work children can do should be linked with sensitive anti-poverty strategies. The structural issues which draw children into work to alleviate low incomes should be tackled.

- **the range of different children's experience of work and the context in which they work.** Any research needs to include an analysis of how gender, ethnic background and disability relate to children's employment. It also needs to take into account issues such as social exclusion, different employment and labour market areas and different locations. In addition, the total lack of baseline data on working children in Northern Ireland needs to be addressed.
- **which aspects of employment are harmful and potentially damaging, and which have a positive impact on children.** Much of the data we have on this is from the United States, and much is out of date. This needs to be sensitive to appropriate age criteria, and include children's perspective.[6]
- **employers' attitudes towards young workers and employers' safety practices;** to develop appropriate ways of improving protection for children who are at risk of accidents.

These recommendations should help set in place effective policies that really benefit working children.

NOTES

1 Non-statistically representative samples.
2 Income data was not collected as part of this project, so direct comparisons are not possible.
3 Low income families are those who are in receipt of income support, see Chapter 3.
4 For example, where families set up informal 'shops' in the home, children and young people often extend their opening hours.
5 See Lavalette, Chapter 2, and Whitney, Chapter 9, for explanation of the laws governing child employment.
6 This links to the ILO work in relation to ILO Convention 138, the Minimum Age Convention.